Hands That Heal

Books by Echo Bodine

Dear Echo
Echoes of the Soul
The Gift
Passion to Heal
Relax, It's Only a Ghost
A Still, Small Voice

Hands That Heal

Echo Bodine

NEW WORLD LIBRARY
NOVATO, CALIFORNIA

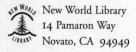 New World Library
14 Pamaron Way
Novato, CA 94949

The material in this book is intended for education. It is not meant to take the place of diagnosis and treatment by a qualified medical practitioner or therapist. No expressed or implied guarantee as to the effects of the use of the recommendations can be given nor liability taken.

The stories in this book are true accounts, but the names of the individuals involved have been changed.

Library of Congress Cataloging-in-Publication Data

Bodine, Echo L.
  Hands that heal / Echo Bodine.— Rev. ed.
     p.   cm.
  ISBN 1-57731-456-5 (alk. paper)
  1. Spiritual healing and spiritualism. I. Title.
  BF1275.F3B63 2004
  615.8'52—dc22   2004003357

First printing, May 2004
ISBN 1-57731-456-5
Distributed to the trade by Publishers Group West

10   9   8   7   6   5   4   3   2   1

This book is dedicated
to everyone who has
taught me about healing.

Contents

Foreword

It's a Saturday morning at the Center — Echo Bodine's healing and teaching center — in Bloomington, Minnesota.

Thirty-two of Echo's students count off by number and then quietly take their places. Some lie on tables padded with fleece quilts handcrafted by Echo. The rest stand next to the tables and begin stretching out their hands. Lit only by candlelight, the room fills with flute music from a Carlos Nakai CD. For the first twenty minutes some students will be the healers, some the healees.

Echo points to a table. She and the class have invited me to receive healing. "Come lie here," she says.

"Not feeling worthy is the biggest barrier to receiving healing," Echo says. "People have so many deep issues with God. They feel if they were really worthy and God was a good God, God would never have given them the illness in the first place. Old religious stuff is the biggest block to receiving healing."

Her words are a healing balm to a voice in my head that nags: *If I hadn't used drugs when I was a kid, I probably wouldn't be dealing with Hepatitis C now, some thirty years later. It's probably my punishment.*

My table is surrounded by healers-in-training. Hands gently touch my shoulders, feet, abdomen — hands resting on top of the white healing hankies that long ago became Echo's trademark. Two of the hands belong to her.

It isn't the first time I have felt this energy; it won't be the last. Sometimes she directly places her hands on me; other times, she sends the energy across the ethers — absentee healings, she calls them — when I ask for help.

"Ec, I'm in Mexico. I either sprained or broke my ankle. I'm trying to make my way to a clinic, but it's an hour away."

"Oh, that's why my hands are heating up," she responds over the telephone. "I just hate it when you're in pain."

"My head hurts so bad," I say, phoning her from California. "I've got a concussion. I know it'll be okay. But I can't even lie down, the pain is so intense."

"My hands are heating up right now," she says. "I'll send you some healing energy. Just go lie down. You should be able to sleep soon."

"For God's sake, do something," I say, grabbing her. "It's my son. Just put your hands on him. Heal him. Please," I beg.

This time she averts her eyes from mine, and she shakes her head. "Shane's gone. His soul left his body. There's nothing I can do. I'm sorry."

When I ask for a healing, I either get the hoped-for results — or I don't.

Now, on this Saturday at the Center, I close my eyes and surrender to the current flowing through the hands. The energy feels golden, light, just warm enough to be comforting. It feels a little like I imagine it would feel if God touched me.

Maybe Echo is right, I think. *Maybe the hardest thing is knowing how loved we are by God.*

After twenty minutes, Echo tells the students it's time to switch places. The healees now become the healers — except for me. I'm invited to continue to receive. At noon, Echo ends the class with a meditation, turns on the lights, and sends us on our way.

"My least favorite thing about being a healer is dealing with all the doubt," Echo confides later, "the 'prove it to me, prove it to me, prove it to me' mentality. My really intellectual students want me to *show* this to them. How do you *show* electricity? You give someone a healing and you see the result."

A few months and several healings later, I'm back at the Center. This time, it's to speak to her students at a New Year's party. The room is filled to capacity. I tell my story of Hepatitis C and the healings. My voice chokes as I finish by sharing that the stubborn viral load count that plagued me has now finally dropped significantly lower than it has ever been. Then I thank the students for their work.

"My favorite thing about teaching healing is watching my students' faces when they hear stories about people getting healed, when it hits them that this stuff really works," Echo says. "It's really sweet."

Over the thirty years I've known Echo, I've watched as the healing energy coming through her hands has grown more powerful. I've also watched as the subject of healing has grown in popularity, working its way from the fringes into mainstream society. What began as classes of six students gathering in the living room of her home has now turned into one hundred new students a year. Some students dream of one day becoming full-time healers; others plan to use this gift more subtly.

"I have a sense that when I retire, I'll hang out my shingle and offer to do healings on others," says one student, a woman who runs a sexual abuse prevention program. "I don't do any official healings in my work. Right now, I practice on myself."

Another woman, formerly an attorney and now a full-time novelist, says she uses her healing gifts for herself and occasionally friends, family, and the characters in her books.

The occupations of Echo's students run the gamut. High school educator, logistics analyst, parent trainer and advocate for parents of youth with disabilities, e-commerce info-tech specialist, and medical office worker alike claim the benefits of learning hands-on healing. Some intend to use this gift to help friends, family, clients, strangers, and pets. Others intend to use it on themselves.

"Many times I go into meetings, and the customers are frightened and angry," says a woman who works as a customer service rep for a community service department. "I'm much more able to be compassionate, patient, even loving now that I'm able to get to a place of centeredness and later clear and heal at the end of the day."

A CEO of three medical companies who is also an electrical engineer says he's been interested in this subject since childhood. "And it's not in conflict with my scientific thinking," he adds.

"I'm filled with awe each time my hands begin to heat up," says another student, one who works as coding specialist for a group of surgeons.

Although I've seen changes in the strength of Echo's healings and in public acceptance of the topic, what I haven't seen change are Echo's beliefs. The same ideas and ideals she wrote about in 1982 when *Hands That Heal* first took on a life of its own are the same ideals she teaches — and lives by — today.

"The people who end up being the best healers are the humble ones," Echo says, "the ones who really work at their connection with God. These are the people who bring through the strong energy because they want to help people and serve God."

In the pages that follow, she'll teach you what hands can do when hearts are tuned to God.

Melody Beattie,
author of *Codependent No More*
and *The Language of Letting Go*

Introduction

Back in 1983, I wrote the first edition of *Hands That Heal*. I have received hundreds of letters from people all over the world thanking me for writing this very simple book on how to channel spiritual healing. Many of you have asked me to let you know if I wrote any more on the subject of channeling healing. Others asked me if there was a way I could teach them more about healing through the mail.

It's been interesting to watch what has been happening in the whole area of spiritual healing in the past decade. My intuition is always reminding me to keep it simple. To get my intellect out of the way and let the Universe work through me. That in itself is very challenging, but I continue to work on it daily.

A part of me shudders when I hear how much some groups or individuals are charging people to learn their "specialized" way of healing. Recently, one of my students told me of a teacher who had given her a list of very rigid rules to live by if she truly wanted to be a spiritual healer. The student was also given a series of prayers to learn before she was allowed to touch others with healing energy and was told she was not to do any healings on anyone until she had taken classes for six months.

Another student told me of a teacher who warned her to stay away from me because I teach about love while this teacher taught about rigidity, fear, and evil. If you've gotten hooked up with someone who is teaching rigidity, using lots of rules or charging you an arm and a leg to learn how to channel healing, I would strongly suggest you ask the Universe to show you quickly the lessons you're there to learn so that you can move on. You don't need this to be a negative experience. Channeling spiritual healing is a wonderful experience. It's joyful. It's loving. It's affordable. It's your birth right as a child of God. And most of all, it's very simple.

The updated information in this book is based on new information I have learned and also on questions many of you have asked me in your letters about charging money for healings, healing ethics and boundaries, clearing, intuition, how to approach someone you think needs a healing, night healing, how to become a stronger channel, the most miraculous healing I've ever seen, and the importance of having a list of resources for your clients.

WHEN I WAS SEVENTEEN years old, I went to a medium for a psychic reading. She told me I was born with the gift of healing and that God would use me as a channel for His healing energy. (For the sake of uniformity, I have used the pronouns "He" and "It" or "Himself" and "Itself" interchangeably when referring to God, realizing that in the spiritual literature of the world the varying concepts of God have been given many different names.)

You may be thinking: "Oh, you lucky girl, how wonderful!" Well, to be truthful, I was pretty upset. I instantly pictured myself running around the country, wearing white robes and being very religious, and never again having any fun — just healing sick people and praying a lot.

I was so confused! I didn't know what to think or what to do. The only healers I had ever heard of were Jesus Christ and Oral Roberts. I felt an overwhelming sense of responsibility that I didn't particularly want.

The medium told me to go home to my father, who was in bed with a migraine headache. She told me to lay my hands on his head. She said God would use my hands as instruments to channel His healing energy to my father.

I remember being so excited, but at the same time feeling like some kind of freak. What would my friends say? How would my boyfriend react? Should I become more religious or start reading the Bible? Should I go to church on a regular basis? But I also fantasized about traveling all over the world healing every sick person I could find. I remember thinking, "I must be special." And the very next thought that followed was, "Why me? I haven't done anything to deserve this."

All of those conflicting thoughts and feelings took place within a thirty-minute drive home that night. Part of me felt grand. Another part felt scared. Another, very responsible, and another, completely in the dark about what to do or how to do it. I wanted God to talk to me about what it all meant.

When I arrived home I told my father what the medium had said. I asked him if I could put my hands on his head. Within a minute, my hands started to heat up like little heating pads. I could actually sense an energy inside. It was slight, and I was sure I was imagining the whole thing. I kept my hands on his head for probably five minutes at the most. (It seemed like five hours!) My hands cooled down to their normal temperature, and it felt like the energy had stopped. I looked at my father, expecting him to tell me I was crazy. But instead, he said his headache was gone.

Almost forty years have passed since that first laying-on-hands healing took place, and I have learned several things through trial and error that I want to pass on to you.

I know God heals. I know the energy will flow through anyone who asks for it. I have felt the energy. I have seen the results. There is nothing complicated about God's healing energy.

There is nothing complicated about God's healing energy. Anyone can be a channel for God's healing energy.

Chapter 1

The Healing Touch

Have you ever noticed your hands becoming unusually warm, or feeling "full," almost as if there's something in them? What I'm describing is healing energy. The sensation is hard to put into words and even harder to explain.

The energy is not always hot. Sometimes the full feeling is so intense, my hands and arms shake or jerk. Sometimes during a healing

❖

God heals people.
God's healing energy flows through us
to heal physical and emotional problems.

❖

my whole upper body feels like it's trembling. My clients each have different ways of experiencing the energy. Some say it feels like bolts of energy flowing through their body. Others say the energy feels like a cool mentholatum going into their body. Some have asked me to take my hands off their bodies because the heat is so intense. Some talk about seeing themselves surrounded in a white light during the healing. Others say they feel pain. Some say they feel nothing. Each client is different. My experience with each client is different, too.

My office

A Healing Session

SOME OF YOU HAVE ASKED me what kind of space is appropriate for doing healings. Before I describe an actual healing session, I would like to describe my office to you. The walls are a very soft yellow with mint green carpeting. I have a couch, chair, and desk on one end of the room, where I sit and talk with clients before our session. At the other end of the room, my healing table is set up, away from walls so that I can walk around it. I have an egg-carton foam-rubber pad on top of the table, covered by a sheet, a pillow for my client's head, and a pillow that fits under their knees to give their legs extra support. To help them relax, I've hung a nature scene poster on the ceiling above the table.

Directly behind the head of the table, I have a stereo with speakers mounted on the wall. I play some type of relaxing music with every session. My intuition guides me as to what music to play, to which of my tapes is best for the particular client and their specific process. Music can actually take people into a process. I had a client who came to heal her broken heart from a previous relationship. I was running my hands over the tapes and felt really pulled to one in particular. I put in the tape, and when it began playing, she said, "Oh no, this reminds me of my old boyfriend." We looked at each other, laughed, and decided that maybe this music was perfect for the healing session. We let the tape play, and it did help to open her heart and release some memories. At the end of the healing, she was grateful she was no longer in the relationship. That was her particular process for the day.

I have candles lit throughout the office and lots of plants in the windows. The furniture and all of the accents in the room are pastel colored. It's a very gentle room. I've put a lot of time and effort into creating an environment in which my clients will feel safe.

I also have several stuffed animals in my office for my clients, young and old, to cuddle with or play with during their session. It is not necessary that clients lie still or stay silent during the healing session. If holding a stuffed animal and listening to the tape *Peter Pan* helps them to relax, that's fine with me. As I said earlier, I make every effort (within reason, of course) to help clients feel comfortable, safe, and as relaxed as possible, so they can open up to receive the healing energy.

Sometimes I feel guided to burn a particular incense, but I don't burn incense every time. Some people don't like it, and some are allergic to it. That's why I need to listen to my intuition and only burn it when I feel guided to do so.

The next subject I would like to discuss before going into the actual healing session is clearing.

❖

Please clear my mind.
Please clear my body.
Please clear my soul.
Thank you.

❖

Clearing

ONE DAY A FRIEND OF MINE, Warren, who is also a channel for healing, stopped by my office. He had never been there before, and because I had just redecorated, I was anxious for him to see the space I worked in. Warren's first comment was, "Oh my god, you need to clear this place. It's full of vibrations from former clients." He said I needed to clear my office after each client left and clear myself after each healing. He also said that before I began a healing, I must clear the client's aura.

At the time Warren visited, my former partner and I were sharing the same office space. I worked three days a week, and she worked three days a week. Warren told me it was very important that we not share the same space because each night angels prepared my work space for my vibration. He said each healer has a different vibration and that it was important that they work in their own space.

I asked Warren how to clear myself, my clients, and the office, and it turned out to be a very simple technique: stand apart from the client and ask the Universe or God to please clear so and so, body, mind, and soul. Then ask that the Universe or God, please clear me, body, mind, and soul. When the client leaves, ask that the office be cleared. Always say thank you, knowing that it has been done.

You may be wondering what we're clearing. Have you ever looked at your clothes at the end of the day and noticed all the lint you've picked up? Well, on a psychic level, we pick up other people's "lint" — their anger, sadness, loneliness, fear, depression, and even their physical problems. We're like little magnets! That's why we need to clear ourselves every day — two, three, four times a day if need be. My psychic teacher told me to clear myself each night before I went to bed so that I would not take the day's "stuff" with me into my sleep. It's hard to get used to doing, but as time has passed, I've gotten better and better at remembering to clear myself, my client, and my healing space when the client leaves. Try it. You'll be amazed at how much better you feel and how open and spacious your healing room feels afterwards.

Two or three days after Warren told me about clearing, two Indian guides appeared to me and told me that sweetgrass was a very good tool for clearing people's auras. ("Guides" refers to friends and helpers who exist on the spirit plane, but are not present in a physical body. They can offer assistance and advice if we are open to asking and to "hearing" a response.) Sweetgrass is an herb made into a braid that can be found in new age bookstores, co-ops, health food stores, et cetera. I hold the braid over a flame (not into it, but over it) and get it to smoke. Then I run the sweet grass down the client's aura, which is about five or six inches above the body. I do not touch the client with the sweetgrass because it could burn them. You just want the smoke of the sweetgrass to run down their aura, clearing them of other people's debris. In this way you know you're working on their healing needs and not everyone else's. Sometimes I have seen this "psychic lint" actually block the healing from going in as deeply as it can, so if it feels like the healing is not going in as deeply as it could, go back and clear the client once again.

I recently did a healing on another healer, and her aura was full of other people's discarded negative energy. When she first lay down on my healing table, she asked me to look psychically and see why people seemed to back away from her when they met her. When I looked at her, she had a haze about three feet wide of other people's pain. I ran sweetgrass up and down her aura for a good three minutes. I told her

Sage burning in an abalone shell

about clearing, and she said she would start doing it before and after each healing from now on.

Another thing that works very well to clear people is crushed sage. I put it in an abalone shell, light it, blow out the fire, and use the smoke to clear, again running the shell up and down the body and about six inches above it. When I do this, I ask God to please clear this person of all the "stuff" they have picked up throughout the day.

To recap: Either before or after your client lies down, run some sweetgrass or sage up and down their aura, or if you prefer, ask your Higher Power to please clear the person, body, mind, and soul. Then before you begin the healing, stand apart from the person and ask that you also be cleared, body, mind, and soul. This is a great time to get centered for channeling the healing.

We all have within us a center, a core. I visualize mine in the area of my solar plexus. I always visualize a white light in that area, and I see that as my connection to God. I take several deep breaths and feel a oneness with the earth. This gives me a feeling of being grounded. I place both feet solidly on the ground. It's very seldom that I wear shoes when I channel healings. I feel more grounded without them. When I'm feeling clear, connected to my center and grounded to the earth, I step up to the person, place handkerchiefs on the areas I will work on, and begin the healing session. After the client has left, I ask the Universe to please clear the office, and I always say thank you, knowing it has been done.

There's one more topic to discuss before we get into the actual healing session, and that is white handkerchiefs.

White Hankies

WHEN THE MEDIUM TOLD ME I was born with the gift of healing, she told me there were two things I was never to forget. One, that it was God who was healing people, that I was simply the channel; and two, always use white handkerchiefs on the area where I'm working. She told me she didn't know why the hankies were so important but that I would understand all of this someday.

I have learned that the hankies absorb and hold positive energy. I had a client from Hawaii who requested absentee healing for a pain in his abdomen. My guides told me to hold a couple of hankies in my hands and channel healing into them. They told me to fold them up, put them in a white envelope, and mail them to my client, instructing him to put the hankies on his abdomen daily until the hankies felt "empty." My guides said he could then mail the hankies back to get more energy in them if he needed it, but they felt it wouldn't be necessary. My client later wrote and told me he thought it was pretty hokey but that he had laid down and put the hankies on his abdomen anyway. He said that within a couple of days of doing this, his pain stopped. Since that time, I have sent several hankies out to people requesting absentee healings. Sometimes I send clients home with the hankies I used during their session, and when they come back for their next healing, they bring the same hankies back. I fill them up with healing energy, and they take them home again, to use whenever they have pain. They always tell me the hankies continue to work. Handkerchiefs also work well for clients who have physical problems that I don't touch directly, such as herpes, prostate problems, hemorrhoids, et cetera. The client puts the hankies directly on the problem when they're at home and tell me they get a lot of relief from their pain.

For practical reasons, the hankies are good to use in the summer because my hands sometimes get sweaty from the heat. The hankies protect the client's clothes from getting moist.

I have heard other healers talk about taking on their client's pain or illness, especially if they are a psychic sponge, which means they absorb other people's emotions, pain, et cetera. I believe the hankies protect me from absorbing my client's mental, emotional, or physical pain.

If I'm out in public and someone needs a healing when I don't have any hankies with me, I use Kleenex or borrow a napkin (if I'm in a restaurant.) I never do a healing without using something under my hands. I strongly suggest you do the same.

Before the Client Comes for a Session

AFTER A NEW CLIENT calls for an appointment, my assistant sends them a letter describing the healing session to help alleviate any fears they may be having. The letter also answers questions they may have about removing clothing (which is never necessary), the length of the session (anywhere from thirty to sixty minutes), and how the healing may release stored emotions or blocked memories and make them feel like crying. I encourage clients to flow with their bodies. If they cry, fall asleep, or feel more comfortable talking, all of it is fine with me. In the letter and at the end of the

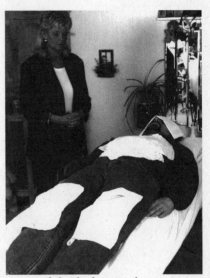

I place hankies on each area where healing will be channeled.

session, I tell them to remain lying on the table until they feel clear-headed and awake. Sometimes if a person gets up too soon, they get lightheaded. I've had some clients sleep up to an hour after their healing, which can sometimes be a problem if I have another client coming right after that session, but it's usually just fine. Almost every time I do have a client who needs to lie for a while longer than anticipated, it ends up that the person coming next is running late or gets lost, so as I said, it usually works out!

People have said they appreciated the letter because it did help them feel more comfortable about coming.

Now to a Healing Session

WHEN CLIENTS ARRIVE, we talk for a while about what it is they would like healed. Some come for physical problems, some for emotional problems, and many for both. When I feel I have gotten the necessary information, I ask them to lie down on the healing table on their back — unless they've come with a back problem, in which case I have them lie on their stomach.

If you don't have a healing table, a bed or couch works just as well. But remember — you are going to be sitting or standing for twenty to forty minutes, so you need to be comfortable, too. If the client is cold, I cover them with a blanket.

Here is a typical step-by-step healing session:

1. As the client lies down and gets comfortable, I'm intuitively picking out the music and lighting the sage or sweetgrass.

2. I wash my hands to get any odor off them and put some lotion on them so they smell nice and feel soft.

3. I lay handkerchiefs on the areas where I plan on doing the healing. I usually start out sitting at their head, placing my hands on each shoulder to send the energy down the entire body and placing hankies on the shoulders, the solar plexus area, and wherever else I'm going to be working.

4. I ask for clearing for my client and myself. I focus on my center. I visualize myself being connected to the earth and

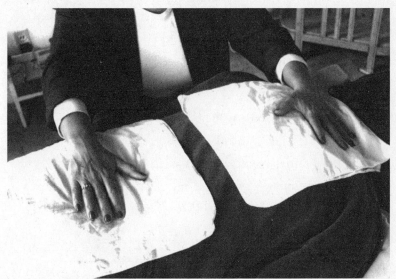

When someone comes with a bad back and it is not too painful for them to lie on their stomach, I work directly on their back.

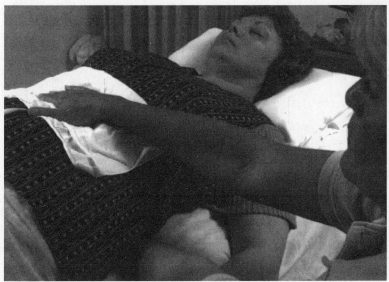

If it is too uncomfortable, I have them lie on their back, and I place one hand on top of their solar plexus and the other where the pain is on their back.

feeling grounded. I focus on my client's body, taking deep breaths until I feel a connection to my client. I ask them if they are comfortable being touched or would prefer I keep my hands above their body.

5. Silently, I say some type of prayer to connect with God, such as the Prayer of Protection. Sometimes I simply thank God for using me as a channel for healing. I ask the energy to move through me to heal my client, and I ask God to direct me with the healing. I feel my oneness with my client and with my Higher Power.

❖

The Light of God surrounds me.
The Love of God enfolds me.
The Power of God protects me.
The Presence of God watches over me.
Wherever I am, God is!

❖

6. I sit at the head of the table, place my hands on the client's shoulders, and move my hands in a counterclockwise circle three or four times to "get into" a deeper level in their body and soul. After about thirty seconds my hands begin to warm up. They may tremble, which is simply the healing energy flowing through. Sometimes my hands will jolt. There will be times throughout the healing when I will move my hands in that counterclockwise circle to go in deeper. I stay in this position for about ten minutes, and

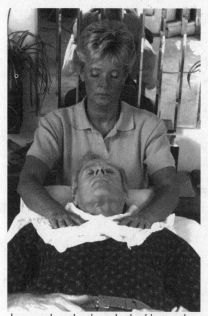

I start with my hands on the shoulders, sending healing down the entire body.

then I move to the specific areas requested. Sometimes I stay at the shoulder area for the entire time.

Throughout the healing I usually remain silent, listening to my inner voice for direction. Sometimes I will get a strong sense to move my hands to areas other than those requested.

Students ask me what I think about during the session. I focus on my intuition for guidance, and I also let my thoughts drift. Yes, it's true! I'm not in a constant prayerful or meditative state. My mind has been known to wander to my grocery list or my plans for after work. I used to feel guilty about not remaining in a constant prayerful or visualizing mode, but I realized it wasn't my thoughts healing the client. It is the healing energy moving through me that heals them.

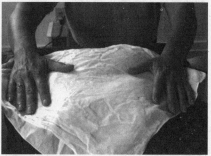

This is the most common position for my hands: one on the upper chest for healing the upper body and the other hand on the solar plexus for healing the lower half of the body.

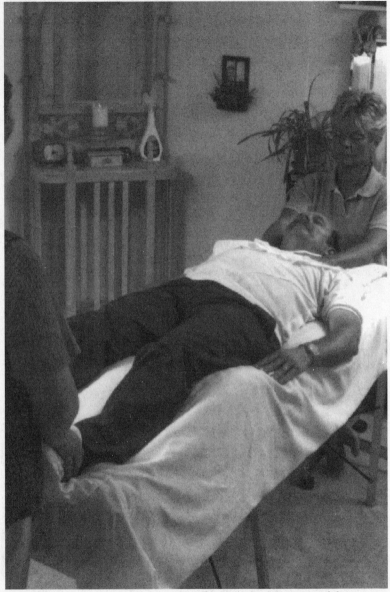

Often my guides or my client's guides will hold the client's feet to ground them
while I channel the healing.

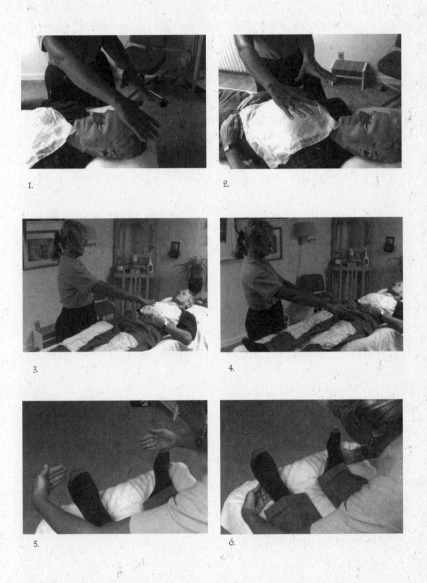

I run my hands down the client's aura, beginning at the head, about four to six inches above the body, smoothing out the aura, and ending at the bottom of the feet.

The length of time for healings has changed over the years. When I first started out, I channeled twenty-minute healings. Today I channel thirty- to sixty-minute healings, depending upon the client and how much their body can handle. Their body lets my hands know when enough is enough, and my hands stop channeling the energy.

On some occasions my hands feel "stuck" to the person, so I just let the energy flow until my hands feel free to move.

7. When the healing feels done, I do two things to end the healing. My hands go in a circle about six inches above the body over and over and over until it feels as if there is an "energy bandage" of protection on the areas just worked. Then I run my hands from the top of the client's head down to their feet again, about four to six inches above the body, smoothing out their aura and ending at the bottom of their feet.

8. I tell them to lie there as long as they want and need to. People usually lie there for five to thirty minutes, depending upon how strong the healing was and how emotional it was for them.

Each time I channel a healing to the same person, it gets stronger and stronger.

9. While they are lying there, "coming to," I shake my hands to release any energy left in them. Sometimes my hands ache after a healing, so I run them under cold water, which seems

to help. I ask God to please clear me, my hands and arms, and my office (after the client leaves).

You may want to give the client a glass of spring water or healing water after they've come to from their healing. It is a good way to help them reconnect with their body and is good for flushing out toxins. I usually encourage my client to drink a lot of water during their healing process.

How to Make Healing Water

TAKE A GLASS PITCHER and fill it up with spring water. Put your hands on the outside of the pitcher and channel healing energy into the pitcher by holding the sides with your hands. I think it is best to channel the energy for at least five minutes, but listen to your intuition also. It will tell you when enough is enough.

I called a reputable healer here in the Twin Cities, Rev. Ron Moor, and asked him how long he thought the water retained the healing energy.

Ron told me he thought it did for at least two to three days, but told me when he does his healing services he makes fresh healing water each time. He suggested checking the water's aura to see if it was still charged, but in my case that wouldn't work because I do not see auras at will. Two to three days felt accurate when he said it, so I trust that's right.

If you happen to make too much healing water, you can water your plants with it, give it to your animals, or drink it yourself. It is simply another form of healing.

Sometimes a client will feel more pain initially after a healing. Even though I'm not 100 percent sure this is the correct answer (and I tell clients this), I say that I believe the healing brought the old pain that's perhaps been stored inside for a long time up to the surface. So far, every client who did experience more pain initially has told me it was usually gone within five to thirty minutes after leaving. Some clients may have flu- or coldlike symptoms, which is an indication of detoxification.

Some clients stop coming if they feel sick, which is a bummer. I wish they would come back and get a healing for the symptoms they are experiencing rather than stop coming altogether. Their bodies are obviously in a healing process, and they need to hang in there with it.

When we are asking for healing for a body, the healing energy may go in and start moving toxins out of the body. For example, if a client complains about flu- or coldlike symptoms while receiving healings, I've found that the symptoms are often the body's way of releasing toxins. This is especially true in someone who has been sick for some time. There's probably a lot of stored pain in their bodies, environmental toxins, allergies, toxins from medicine, and other toxins.

The intention of the healing energy is to heal, but we don't know how that healing is going to manifest. Back in 1979, I belonged to a weekly prayer group. I was having a lot of problems with my colon, which I had had all of my life. Each week I prayed for healing. It seemed to continually get worse, not better. I got healings from a healer friend of mine and would get some short-term relief and then the pain was back. I ended up in the hospital and had surgery on my colon. I felt betrayed by God because He didn't heal my colon and here I was in the hospital, having my second colon surgery. A voice said to me, "You prayed for a healing on your colon, and it is now healed."

The doctor had told me that it looked like I had been born with a floppy (weak) colon and that was why I had had problems all my life. He cut out thirteen inches and told me I wouldn't have any more problems. And I haven't, but the point of the story is that sometimes there's more to our healing process than just receiving healing energy.

You may want to share with a client who has come with a head cold, bronchitis, emphysema, or asthma that they may cough or sneeze a lot after healing. The healing may go in and loosen everything up in order for the body to release what's stuck inside.

I tell clients to see how they feel from the healing and, if they would like to come for another appointment, to call me back to set something up. I always make sure they are fully awake when they leave. Some feel very energized after a session; some are very relaxed. Depending on how strong the healing was, they may be very spacey when they come out of the session, so make sure they are clearheaded and ready to drive.

Sometimes I have a client who goes out deeply during the session and is sound asleep for quite a while. If this happens for you, check the client's breathing. If it is very shallow and if their body appears very still, chances are they are astral projecting, which means that their soul is outside the body. Don't shake them or yell at them to wake up. If you do have someone else coming and need the healing space, silently speak to the client's soul and tell it that you need them to come back into the body. Then leave the client alone. It will be coming back shortly. If you roust them too quickly, they can be very disoriented when they wake up. If you don't need your healing space right away, just leave them alone. The soul will be back in their body as soon as it is done doing whatever it is doing. Don't panic. Souls leave the body quite often, so it's not any reason to be frightened.

What to Do If They Feel "Stuck"

SOMETIMES YOU MAY FEEL a client is "stuck," like their body isn't taking in much or has stopped letting healing in. There are several things you can do in this situation:

- Tell the client to take a deep breath and blow it out. Do it again and again, until you feel the block move.

- Sometimes the healing energy moves buried emotions and/or blocked memories to our conscious mind. Our body can sense we're about to become conscious of an old stored feeling or memory that we've kept hidden away for a long time, and oftentimes, this brings up fear. Fear causes blocks to healing quite often. Taking a deep breath, or several, and blowing it out of the body can actually move the fear or whatever the block is.

- Another technique my guides taught me is to have the client visualize a zipper running from their throat to their solar plexus. Tell them to visualize unzipping this zipper. This helps them open up to the healing. After your client has done either of these techniques, your hands may channel stronger healing energy. That's because the blocks have moved or they've opened up to receive more. Be sure to have them visualize zipping up the zipper when you are done with the healing.

NOT EVERYONE NEEDS these techniques. I only suggest them when the person feels "stuck." What does stuck feel like? It feels like there's a wall up between the client and your hands. It feels like the energy is backing up into your hands. It feels like there is no flow. You sense it more than you can intellectualize it. Just remember to stay tuned in to your intuition, and you'll have a sense of what to do throughout the healing.

Absentee Healings

ABSENTEE HEALINGS are healings that take place when you, the channel, are not in the presence of the person receiving the healing. Here's what I do when I'm sending an absentee healing.

I sit down. I center on the person who has asked for the healing. I visualize the healing taking place as if they were right in front of me. I ask God to please heal so-and-so. I wait until I feel a "connection" with the person. It's an intuitive feeling. Then I say "thank you" knowing that the healing is taking place, and I either go on to the next person on my list or go on about my day. My part takes between two and five minutes, depending upon how long it takes for me to feel the connection.

Absentee healing does work. Whenever someone calls with a healing need and you are not able to get to them, tell them you can send absentee healings. I'm a night owl, so I usually channel healing late at night when the client is in bed. Many times I pray for absentee healing twice a day for someone. You'll have to decide what's best for you and what fits in with your schedule.

You should tell the client they may experience the warmth or tingles of the healing energy. I've had many clients report back to me that they felt the heat or the tingling. Some have said they could feel hands on their body.

I have received numerous calls and letters from clients over the years letting me know they began to experience the healing energy immediately after calling and making a request for absentee healing. As

I have said earlier, the healing energy is universal. The process begins as soon as a person asks — which indicates they have opened themselves up to the healing energy. You might be wondering, "Couldn't I just pray for absentee healing for everyone who calls for a healing, rather than see people in person?" Yes, you could.

Here is another form of healing:

Night Healings

A FEW YEARS AGO my psychic teacher called and told me I was doing a lot of my healing work at night in my sleep. She told me a woman called her to tell her that after reading my book, she sat on the edge of her bed one night and asked me to please come to her and give her a healing. She said she woke up in the middle of the night and saw me standing over her with my hands on her, healing her body. She said she woke up the next day with no more pain!

Over the last few years, I've heard similar stories from several people.

I've also had people tell me I came to them during the day to give them healing. I tracked a couple of the stories back to the day and time of the healing, and at the exact day and time, I was home lying down taking a nap.

A few weeks ago, I had a client call about her son who had a very bad cold. She needed to get him in right away, and I was all booked, so I thought I'd give night healing a conscious try. When I went to bed, I asked my soul if she would go to little Matthew's house and give him a healing. When I woke up in the morning, I asked myself if I went to Matthew's house. I had a vision of Matthew lying in his bed; his heart was broken (emotionally) by someone the previous week, but he was physically better. I asked my assistant to call and verify if Matthew had

had an emotional upset in the last week and if he was feeling any better. His mother told my assistant that she had had a dream that I came to visit them in their home. She said Matthew was much better physically and that yes, some playmates had really hurt his feelings badly and also that his father, who had been visiting them, left and went back East. Matthew was having a hard time getting over both of these hurts.

Once my intellect got past the "you've got to be kidding" stage and sank down into my inner knowingness, I knew that it was true. My soul was leaving my body and was channeling healings to people who were calling out on a soul level.

I started thinking back, and there were many times I would get unusually tired in the afternoon and would lie down for a quick nap. I could feel my soul lift away from my body, and I would blank out. Then about twenty to thirty minutes later, I would feel my soul pop back in, and I'd be wide awake. I knew my soul had been gone, but it never occurred to me I was out doing healings. I used to get upset with myself about taking naps during the day because I thought I was being lazy.

My attitude has changed quite a bit. It makes sense to me that because I love what I do and feel a real dedication to my work that it isn't just limited to the hours when I'm awake or to how much my body can do.

It's very exciting work when you realize how unlimited we really are. And to take it a step further, think about all the healing going on for our souls when we're sleeping.

Doing Healings in Hospitals

I'VE GONE TO HOSPITALS many times to channel energy, and over the years I've learned it's best to keep what you're doing between you and your client. I used to take my hands off my client whenever anyone from the medical staff walked in the room, but now I continue to touch them, just not in a conspicuous way.

Sitting by their side touching their arm or holding their hand will work just as well as working right on the spot in need of healing. In this way you avoid needing to get into a conversation with anyone about what you're doing or being put in a position where you feel defensive.

Sometimes the person receiving the healing tells the nursing staff that you're there to channel healing, and hopefully, if they don't have a problem with this, you can just do your work.

You may be surprised to find out how many medical people have a pretty negative attitude about spiritual healing. Some think we're setting people up with false hopes. Some think we're con artists or religious fanatics.

I have been treated so rudely by some nurses that I no longer offer any information to them about what I'm doing unless they seem really open to hearing about spiritual healing. I don't want to give nurses a bad rap here because I have a lot of respect for the hard work they do and for their sense of dedication. Maybe I've just run into an unusually high number of nurses who do not believe in healing, and maybe there are many of them out there who do believe in it. The point of this is that I strongly suggest you do your work in as inconspicuous a way as possible without setting yourself up for criticism or ridicule. You don't need it. You don't deserve it. (I would not recommend bringing candles, incense, or sage to a hospital. Besides the fact that there are canisters of oxygen everywhere that may ignite, you aren't allowed to light matches in the rooms.) Remember: INCONSPICUOUS.

The other reason for not attracting attention to yourself as a healer is that it could jeopardize the relationship between the patient and the nursing staff.

When my sister was in the hospital and I was channeling healing to her, we did not tell the doctors or nurses because we did not want them to treat my sister like she was crazy for believing in this.

I know times are changing, and with so many nurses learning Therapeutic Touch (a form of healing), we may soon be able to go into hospitals and be open about what we're doing. But until that time comes, we need to be discreet in order to protect ourselves and the client.

Astral Projection

I HAVE ALREADY TOUCHED on astral projection in a couple of different places in this book. While working on someone in a hospital, you'll run into this more than you will when seeing clients in your healing space.

Astral projection is when the soul leaves the body and travels. There are many reasons why a soul goes out from the body, but when it comes to illness/disease, the soul leaves the body to give the body a break. When the soul is out of the body, the body usually does not feel pain.

It is very simple to tell if the client is in or out of their body. Is the body completely still? Is the breathing very shallow? Do they almost appear dead? If these things are happening, the soul is out of the body. It may be out of the hospital, hovering over the body or standing out in the family room with the family listening to what's going on.

I like working on a body when the soul is out because the body lies very still and the healing goes in deeply. When the soul is in, the body thrashes around in pain, and it's hard for the body to relax and let the healing in.

Many times I start out channeling the energy while the soul is still in, i.e., the person is talking, moving around, breathing normally. After a few minutes, the person becomes very relaxed, and many times falls into a deep sleep.

If this happens when you're channeling a healing to someone in their home or a hospital, just let them be. Don't try to make them be in their body. Don't keep them awake by constantly talking to them. Let the soul and the body take a break while you're working. If the soul is still gone when you're finished channeling the healing, just leave them be and go home. The soul always finds its way back to its own body. You're not responsible for making that happen.

Chapter 2

Not Everyone
Is Ready to Be Healed

Not everyone is ready to be healed. Hard to believe? I know. It was hard for me to believe that everyone who is sick is not ready to be healed. But if you're going to be a channel for healing, you need to accept that some don't want or aren't ready for healing. The fact is we can't interfere in other people's lives. Just because we may believe they would be happier or better off if they were healed doesn't make it true.

Once you discover you have the gift of healing, I think the natural tendency is to want to do healings on everyone you know who is sick or in pain.

I understand that desire to help others, but we can't just barge into people's lives thinking we know what's best for them, or that we know what they want or need.

People have gotten turned off to spiritual healers because some have been very pushy. They push their beliefs on people, push the healing on people, and that's not right.

Here's what you need to do when you become aware of someone who is sick or in pain:

1. Tell them you are a channel for healing and that you would like to channel a healing to them if that's what they would like. Ask them to think about it and give you a call.

2. *Don't stand there waiting for their answer.* Don't pressure them! You may have just "blown their mind," and they may need time to think about what you have just said. They may have known you for years and not known you were a healer. It may be a little unsettling to them at first.

News like this may bring up different issues for people. Some may not even know if they believe in spiritual healing. Some may have issues with God they don't necessarily want to look at. Some may have worthiness or self-esteem issues and may not feel worthy of being healed. Some may believe God gave them this illness/disease as punishment for something, so they don't believe God will heal them.

Whatever the reasons, whether conscious or subconscious, don't pressure them. Let them come to you. A story comes to mind of a good friend of mine, a minister, who died a few years ago. When he was diagnosed with cancer, he asked me not to tell anyone in the congregation. He feared once it got out in the church that he was sick, that he would have every healer in the place knocking on his door wanting to give him healings. Word got out somehow, and that's exactly what happened. He told me he had some very insistent healers telling him their way was the only way and that they needed to do healings on him. Who are we to say our way is the *only* way? We can't push our will on anyone. If people feel *safe* with us, they'll come to us, when and if they are ready.

Once again, tell them that you channel spiritual healing and that you would like to channel a healing to them if they would like to do that. Ask them to give it some thought and give you a call. Then the hard part for us is to *detach!* Walk away. Leave it alone! If it's meant to be, they will call. Don't take it personally if they don't call. People get sick for many, many reasons. We probably won't know all the reasons until we get to the other side and can see more objectively.

Remember how in the Bible Jesus asked people if they wanted to be healed? I used to think that was kind of a dumb question, but I no longer do. It's a simple question, but the reasons for it are very important, and not always so simple.

There are several reasons people get sick, and while I'm certainly not an authority on the whys of illness, I will pass on to you some of the reasons I have come to understand. Some of the reasons discussed here may be operating as unconscious motivators more than as conscious choices. Either way, they are important.

"Reasons" for Illness

- Our culture has in the last few years gotten much better about allowing us to take "mental health" days off work, but there are still some of us who believe we have to do an "honest" day's work, five days a week, no matter what. The only excuse for not doing what we perceive as "our share" is to be sick. So, we get sick! We get a day or two off. We get well and go back to work.

- I have met children who have learned that the only way to get the nurturing attention or tenderness they need is by being sick. I have also met several adults like that.

- There are people who are learning some valuable lessons through their illness, and these lessons are important for their soul's development.

I believe that a high percent of all illness starts with an emotion or a memory that is stuck within the body. It could be hurt feelings, anger, fear, resentment. It could be a lack of forgiveness of ourselves or others. It could be self-hatred, or wanting to punish ourselves or someone else. Some people react to the unfairness in life by subconsciously creating illness. When I have a health challenge myself, the first thing I do is talk to my emotions. I ask my body what it is that the illness is trying to tell me. Am I holding in some emotions that I need to express? If I'm willing to know the answer, it will always come. If I don't get a clear message, I look at the specific body-part that is in pain. I think about what it might symbolize.

Here are some examples of what I'm talking about when I say an illness can symbolize something.

Eye Problems: What is going on in my life that I am not seeing clearly, or don't want to look at?

Ear Problems: What's being said to me that I don't want to hear?

Throat Problems: Is there something I want to say to someone that I am holding back? Do I find something in my life "hard to swallow"?

Get the idea? I keep it as simple as possible. I don't believe it's always as simple as some of the above examples, though. These examples are meant only to indicate that illness has its own kind of meaning or language much of the time, and knowing that can help us in healing ourselves and our clients.

My second book, *Passion to Heal,* takes an in-depth look at the relationship between unresolved emotional issues and health problems. I highly recommend this book for someone dealing with a health challenge. It can be a very helpful tool in their healing process. I also recommend the book to all health-care practitioners, teachers, therapists, and the clergy because it covers a wide variety of emotional issues that can turn into physical problems.

When we "stuff" our emotions, either by denying them or minimizing them, they stay "stuck." Our feelings do what they can to be released, but when we're not cooperating with that releasing process, the emotions start working away at the physical body. Sometimes they are stored up for years; sometimes the physical aches and pains come shortly after emotional pains have occurred that were not expressed.

I've come to see how deadly stored anger can be. Many people I have seen have stored resentments since childhood. Fear is another devastating emotion. Seventeen years ago I had surgery to correct blockages in my colon. Through hypnosis I saw my colon was filled with fears. I think this is because most of my life I have felt awkward about expressing emotion. I have stored most of them up and have learned firsthand how devastating their effects on the body can be. Needless to say, and awkward or not, I am learning to express my emotions!

Don't assume that anyone with a physical problem is ready for, wants, or would have a healing.

- I have met people with physical problems who do not feel worthy of being healed. They believe sickness is a punishment they deserve from God.

- There are those who have been sick for so long or who have grown so dependent on illness to get them what they want, that the thought of functioning in a healthy body and learning the new lifestyle this would require is too threatening.

- Another area to consider when working with illness is karma. Each of us is a unique child of God. Each of us has our own path to follow in this lifetime, and depending upon what we've been up to in our past lives, there are certain experiences we may need to have in order to learn and grow spiritually.

Always remember: don't force your will on anyone! It is very important to the healing process that the person suffering ask for the healing themselves. You can let the person know you channel healing energy, but leave it up to them to ask for it.

Another important thing to remember:

❖

Don't judge anyone's illness or their reasons for being ill.

❖

We human beings want to know the "whys" of everything. Many people on a "spiritual path" judge illness as "failure." They feel any physical problems are signs of emotional/mental/spiritual dis-ease.

If life is truly a learning experience and we come here to experience all aspects of life, then perhaps some people are experiencing physical handicaps or illness as an ultimate "challenge" to overcome. Or, perhaps a physical ailment presents an individual with the opportunity to more easily go inward and concentrate on the other sides of life. Or, an illness may assist the person in developing empathy, patience, or a number of other attributes. It is not our job to judge — either ourselves or another party. We are responsible only for ourselves and can choose healing if we wish.

Chapter 3

How Long Does It Take
to Be Healed?

Before we look at how long healing takes, we need to look at another important question: what does "healing" mean? I think we all assume that getting healed means being restored to perfect health. But healing could mean many different things, for example:

- Emotional issues could be healed instead of the body.

- The soul could be healed, giving the person a feeling of release and liberation from old issues and beliefs.

- Physical pain may heal while underlying disease may remain. For example, AIDS clients have told me that the healings took away their pain and greatly improved the quality of their lives, but they still died from the disease.

- Sometimes a client will come with a specific healing need and another part of their body will be healed instead. (A client who came for a healing of her eyes later told me her chronic constipation stopped after one healing but her eyes stayed the same! In fact, because she had come for her eyes and not the constipation, she felt she hadn't received a healing.)

Can you see how healing means different things to different people?

It's also important to consider that physical problems can be karmic and contain profound learning lessons for the soul. I had a client who was nine months old. He was born with cancer of the eyes. I took him for a walk and asked his soul to please talk to me about the cancer and tell me what he wanted from the healing. I knew his parents wanted the boy healed of cancer, but the soul always has its own agenda. His soul did tell me that he had chosen this body and that he knew it had cancer when he entered it. He told me he needed to be blind in one eye to learn the life lessons of a partially blind person, but asked me to please heal the left eye, as it only had a little cancer in it and it wasn't necessary for him to be completely blind. So I worked on the left eye. I never saw the boy again, but his mother did call me a month later to tell me that while her son had lost sight in his right eye, all of the spots of cancer in his left eye disappeared after our healing.

ANOTHER AREA OF HEALING that we often fail to discuss is death. For a long time, when a client died, I felt like I had failed as a healer. That's silly. We all die. We need to exit this planet somehow.

There is a very strong survival instinct within each of our bodies. Our bodies do not give up easily. They want to live. The problem here is each of us dies. Because we fight so hard to live, some of us go through absolute physical hell in our dying process.

If a client is in their dying process, they are not going to get better long term. I have met some clients who were dying who did get better temporarily so they could accomplish a few more things before they left. I had one client, thirty years old, dying of liver cancer. The healings gave her a boost of energy and strength and took away the physical pain for about three weeks. She was like a new woman. She planted a perennial garden. She met with friends she hadn't seen in a long while. She went shopping at her favorite mall. She did all the things she told herself she was going to do when she got better, until she suddenly took a turn for the worse and died very quickly. I was devastated because I thought she was healing. We all did. Realistically, she was healing. She was finishing up loose ends, and when she died, it was a healing for her soul. She was free.

There is no way healers can predict how a person's healing process is going to go. I am constantly reminded that my job as their healer is to assist them in whatever process they're in. I can't know for certain what they need to experience from their illness or disease and need to trust that they are getting exactly what they need from our healing.

In almost every healing I have channeled, a process seems to take place within the client. If you are going to use your healing gift, you need to be patient with this process. The process is unique for each person. Clients may connect with themselves in a deeper way. They may release old emotions, old blocks, old memories — memories from past lives, or memories from this lifetime. They may work on forgiveness, self-doubt, self-hate, self-love, resentment, anger, and letting go, or they may experience a purely physical healing. The healing process is individualized; no two healings are alike.

It helps to stay as emotionally detached as you can. Don't get in there and try to hurry up the process. As I said earlier, we are each on our own path, going at our own pace, for a reason.

Now that we've covered what healing might mean to different people, let's look at how long it takes to be healed.

Almost every time I channel energy to someone, they want to know how many visits it will take before they are healed. When I began to channel healing, Jesus Christ was the only Healer I had ever read about. Since all of His healings appeared to be instantaneous, I wondered why it was that some people I worked with weren't healed instantly.

For a long time I feared I lacked something. I tried all kinds of things, thinking there was something wrong with me that kept my clients from getting instantly healed. I went through various phases. I cut out red meat, sugar, and caffeine. I quit smoking cigarettes and stopped swearing. Eventually, I realized that it wasn't about what I, the channel for healing, was doing. It was about the clients and the process they needed to go through. It's really not about the channel. It's about the client's process.

A client recently came to me with cancer, arthritis, low thyroid, a sluggish colon, and bad eyesight. Her comment as she was getting up on my healing table was "I better not have to come back here. You better get this job done today. This is a real drag for me to have to come here." When her thirty-minute healing was over, she said she didn't feel any better and felt she had been ripped off!

People spend years and years getting sick. They don't address their physical issues as they come up, hoping that they will go away, while unresolved emotional issues eat away at the body causing all kinds of problems. Many people then blame God, the medical establishment, or other health-care practitioners when they aren't instantly "fixed."

If a client asks you how many sessions they will need, explain to them that there is no way for you to know how many sessions they will need. They may have to come back several times, or they may be healed after the first session. Some people believe that healing is hard work and therefore takes a lot of time and effort. They might also believe that the more serious the ailment, the more time it *should* take to heal. Some people are working on liking themselves well enough to allow healing. It can take time for them to achieve sufficient self-love. Some clients experience "secondary gains" from being ill (such as gaining attention, getting out of doing something they dislike, receiving disability payments, or taking medication that gets them high) and resist healing (usually unconsciously) until ready to give up their payoffs. Illness can feel safe and familiar. Healing is a change, and even when we know a change is for the better, it can feel frightening. Given all of these variables, it's impossible to predict how long healing will take.

It is also important to understand that some clients think their role in healing is a passive one. This type of client, like my client mentioned earlier, thinks it's all our responsibility to get them well. It doesn't occur to them to take an active role in their healing process; they simply want you to fix them — now!

Beware of this and watch that you don't become caught up in what I call the "Savior Set-up." You are not their savior. You are not responsible to heal them instantly or in ten sessions. There may be an agenda going on for them somewhere. It could be emotional, physical, or karmic, and you or I don't know what it is. One thing I am clear on is:

❖

People are healed when they are ready to be healed!

❖

Chapter 4

You Have Your Own
Inner Helper

Within your body, somewhere between your heart and the middle of your body, there is a voice.

The Bible refers to this voice as the "still small voice within." This gentle voice is your intuition.

I think intuition has gotten a bum rap. Many of us tend to minimize it, thinking it's some wacky women's thing. But the truth is both men and women have it, and it is a voice that is always there for us, wants to help us, and is 100 percent accurate when it does guide us.

How many times have you been in a very difficult situation and begged God to talk to you, to help you? You waited for a thundering voice from on high and when it didn't come, you felt abandoned. Maybe you even took it a step further and decided God wasn't there for you — or that there was no God.

So many of us desperately want God to shout to us from the Heavens or put the writing on the wall when we're hurting, but my minister once said (and I hated it), "God doesn't shout. God whispers.

41

Our job when faced with a crisis is to calm ourselves, go within, and listen for the gentle voice inside."

Somehow it doesn't seem fair that when we're all riled up and upset, we have to calm ourselves in order to hear God, but the truth is we do need to do that.

I truly believe that the soft, gentle voice inside each of us is God's voice. It's easy to feel abandoned when we're upset, but truthfully, we aren't.

If you have never worked on listening to your inner voice, I'll offer these suggestions to help you tune in to it. Get a copy of my book *A Still, Small Voice* and read it several times. Do the exercises and follow the suggestions at the end of each chapter. Don't be in a hurry. This book will change the way you see life, yourself, and God.

There are so many reasons why it's important to learn to hear your intuition:

- It helps you live your life so much more easily. It cuts out half the legwork because when you ask daily for guidance, you will be given it.

- It guides you in your work as a healer — and in any line of work. But because we often work alone as healers, it is especially helpful to hear that inner voice. The guidance can be quite specific, such as, *"Move your hands here; put your right hand over there; say this to the person; ask them this; stop the channeling; continue the channeling; have the client come back twice this week — five times this week — once every two weeks."* This kind of guidance comes from God and is quite helpful. If we listen, it's there!

- You no longer feel alone or abandoned by God. When you hear that voice inside, you feel loved and supported.

- Your relationships with other people change, your parenting changes, and even your relationships with animals change, because you feel connections that are impossible to feel when you live only in your head.

I'd like to do an exercise with you to help you know the difference between your intellect and your inner voice.

Close your eyes. Focus on your solar plexus (where your belly button is). Ask your intuition, "Are you there?" You will feel an inner nudging.

Pay attention to the area you're focusing on. Are you focusing on your head?

One of my students recently asked me, "How do I know if it's my head talking to me or my intuition?" Very simply, focus on where the information is coming from. If you're in your head, you'll be focusing there. If it's your intuition, you will be focusing on your middle.

If you're feeling muddled up inside, ask the Universe to please clear you so you can "sense" what the silent voice is saying.

I'm going to ask you some questions, and I want you to focus on your intuition. Ready? *(Answers on next page.)*

1. Is Echo's living room painted light green or pink? When you say light green or pink, you will feel a slight nudging inside when you get the right answer.

2. Next question: Was Echo's last pet a cat or a dog? Feel the answer, get out of your head. If you can't get an answer, ask the question again. Was Echo's last pet a cat or a dog?

3. Is Echo a vegetarian? Yes or no?

4. Does Echo have any children? Yes or no?

5. Does Echo like to water ski? Yes or no?

ARE YOU FOCUSING ON YOUR INTUITION? When you hit the correct answer it feels right. You just *know* the answer is right.

One of the reasons we as healers need to develop our intuition is for our work. I rely on my inner voice to guide me in my healing work every day. It guides me in what music to play during each client's healing session. It tells me where to place my hands, when to talk, and when to be silent. I am directed toward how long I need to channel, how long to leave a client alone after the healing, and toward how often the client needs to come, which varies from once a week, to every other week, to once a month.

Intuition has integrity. It's not going to run a scam on people or tell them they need to come every day so you or I can get that new refrigerator! If a client needs to come every day, you will "hear" or know that intuitively, but you won't hear it just because you *want* to hear it. Intuition always has the client's best interests in mind. It knows what they need. It will also have your best interests in mind and will know how much channeling your body can handle.

The other reason we as healers need our intuition is to guide us in everyday life. Oftentimes healers are self-employed. We work by ourselves. There's no boss around to lay down the rules, or the hours we work, or the days we can take off. We are it!

Answers: 1. Green 2. Dog 3. No 4. Yes 5. No

Being in the healing business is rough. Some weeks my workload is full and steady. Other weeks, there are holes in my schedule, and as healers we can't exactly go out and solicit business. We build up a good reputation, and usually, through word of mouth, the business comes in.

Intuition helps with finances as well. Let me give you an example of how my intuition helps me in this regard. My appointment book is all booked for the week coming up. I'm out shopping on my day off. I see a pair of earrings I really want, but instead of just buying them, thinking that I've got a full week of clients coming so these earrings won't hurt my budget, I ask my intuition if it's okay to buy them. If I get a yes, great! If I get a no, I listen. I've learned the hard way to listen to my intuition first and my wants second. It doesn't mean my clients are necessarily going to cancel, but what it does mean is that an expense may come up during the week that I don't know about yet. It doesn't necessarily mean something bad is going to happen when my intuition says no. It could mean I will find some nicer earrings along the way!

I even pay my bills by intuition (which used to drive my husband — now ex-husband — crazy!) I ask my intuition to show me in what order to pay the bills. Yes, I do try to get the bills in by their due date, but again, I listen to my intuition. For some of you, this is going to sound bizarre, and perhaps it is. But my point is this: the Universe knows what's coming up. I don't. It knows what my real schedule is going to be, how my body's energy is going to be, which events of the coming week may cause more stress than I'm aware of. It knows about all the expected and unexpected events. It has my best interests in mind. It always steers me in the direction that's best for me. It works!

When you wake up in the morning, ask your intuition to guide you throughout your day. Ask it if there's anything you should do. Try to stay out of your head! Let ideas flow to you. Perhaps while you're in the shower or on your way to work or school, be open and stay aware of ideas or inspirations that may come to you.

Developing a relationship with your intuition is really fun. Once you get rolling with it, it sometimes feels like you've got this huge "in" as to how life really works. (You do!) You no longer feel alone or so confused. You'll still be confused on occasion because the intuition sometimes gives us a "wait" or "later" answer. But even then there's a peacefulness, the sense that while we may not have gotten the answer we wanted, we did get the right one.

I can give you guidance in this book about being a healer, but your real helper will be your intuition — that feeling, that inner knowing, that hunch, a sense.

I used to say to God, "Why didn't you give me a manual with this gift? Why do I have to figure it all out by myself?"

The good news is we don't have to figure it out all by ourselves. We have an internal knowingness that guides us twenty-four hours a day.

Please work on developing a relationship with your intuition and on trusting it to guide you. You won't believe how wonderfully the gifts of healing and intuition work together. It's amazing how easy it all becomes.

Chapter 5

Healing Ethics
and Boundaries

This topic is very important because as healers we are responsible for creating a safe environment for our clients, a place where they can do their healing work.

If you do this work, you will see the variety of physical and emotional problems that people suffer. You are likely to witness clients on your healing table going through a range of emotional processes. The majority cry. Some get images of abuse done to them in their childhoods or in a past life. Some get very angry and yell or scream during their session. Some kick their legs or pound their fists on the table. Some smile throughout the entire session because the energy feels so nurturing. Reactions vary depending upon how connected the client is to their body, their emotions, and their soul.

We want to create an atmosphere in which clients feel safe enough to do whatever emotional work their healing requires. For instance, our touch needs to be firm enough so that clients feel safe and even protected by us, but not so firm that it hurts them or they feel pain.

I once went to a healer who rocked his hands back and forth on my stomach so much that I felt sick after the healing. His hands were pressing down very hard, and the rocking motion was painful. I couldn't wait to get out of there! I didn't say anything because I thought maybe this was a special technique he used. Whether it was or wasn't, I chose not to go back because it made me feel sick and I didn't feel safe.

Next, we have to be very careful where and how we place our hands. This is a very important boundary, and I think it's even more important for all you male healers. We cannot be sexual with our clients in any way. We have to respect people's physical boundaries. Women's breasts, heart problems, herpes, vaginal problems; men's prostate gland problems, genital disorders, hemorrhoids, sexually transmitted diseases — these can all be worked on without touching these parts of the body. There is one standard healing position, which has already been illustrated in chapter 1.

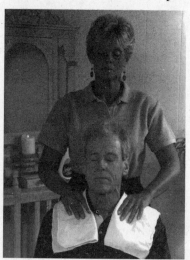 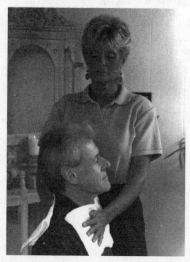

If you prefer to stand, here are two different positions you can work in.

If your client is lying down, place one hand on the upper chest area by the throat and the other hand on the solar plexus, which is the area where our belly buttons are. The healing energy will go wherever it needs to go. If your client is sitting in a chair, you can stand behind them and place your hands on their shoulders, or place one hand in front on their chest and the other on their back and channel the energy down to their entire body.

> We as healers need to be very clear
> with ourselves about our boundaries —
> what we're willing to do and not do.

Open communication helps a great deal. You can ask your client if they would like to be touched or if they would prefer you keep your hands above the body.

A story comes to mind of a client who came to me for healing of the scar tissue inside her breasts from reconstructive surgery. I didn't ask her if she preferred that I place my hands directly on the scarred area. I just kept my hands about three to four inches above her body, which some healers do all the time. (Some healers never touch the body.)

I could feel this client's disappointment that I hadn't placed my hands directly on her breasts. My own discomfort at touching another woman's breasts had stopped me from doing so. Some people feel that if the healing area isn't directly touched, the healing won't be as effective. This client never returned, and this stuck in my mind. I wish I had dealt with the issue differently, perhaps dealt with it straight on instead of avoiding it. I did learn something from the experience, though.

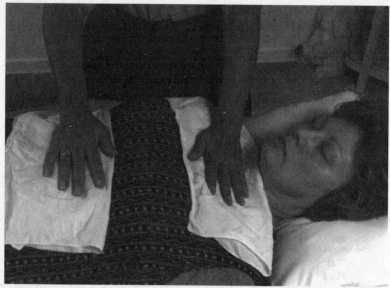

For breast, heart, or lung problems, you can place one hand
above the breasts and one below the breasts.

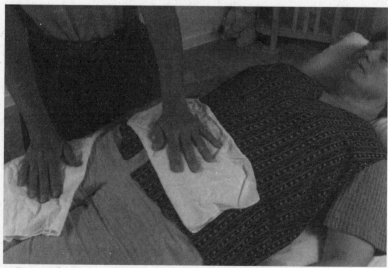

For conditions such as herpes, prostate gland disorders, hemorrhoids, and genital problems,
I sometimes put one hand on the pelvis area and one hand on the upper leg,
asking the energy to go wherever it needs to.

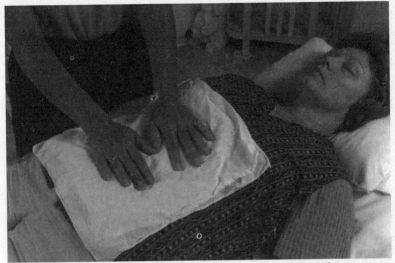

Other times, I put both hands on the solar plexus and, again, ask the Universe to send the healing energy where it needs to go.

Another client, a man with severe bleeding hemorrhoids, wanted me to put my hands directly on his hemorrhoids. He was adamant about it, but it was completely unnecessary. I placed one hand on his lower back, the other on his lower abdomen and asked the energy to go where it needed to go. He was not happy with me, and he told me he did not think the healing would work without direct touch. I told him that was not true, that the energy would go right to the problem regardless of whether it was touched directly or not.

After our session was over, I asked him if he wanted a referral to another healer, and I did refer him to a male healer. Unfortunately, I never found out if my healing helped him or if he ever went to see another healer.

I've had a few male clients who have been disappointed with me for not directly touching their problem area. I'm simply not comfortable placing my hands on their prostate glands or herpes or genitals for problems of impotency. As a healer, I have to feel as comfortable as my client.

This next story is an example of my *not* touching the affected area and yet still giving the client exactly what she needed. I was at a Spiritual Frontiers Fellowship conference in Detroit, Michigan, with my friend Alberto Aguas in 1988. We were up on stage with several other healers. There were at least 150 people lined up to come up to the stage, sit in a chair, and get a healing from one of several of us channeling healing. A woman sat in my chair, and I placed my hands on her head and asked the energy to go where it needed to go. After only five minutes, the woman told me she had a lot of problems with vaginal bleeding and could feel all the warmth from my hands going to her vagina. I saw her the next day, and she said the bleeding had stopped. My point: we don't have to touch the affected area in order to bring about a healing.

We can — and must — maintain safe boundaries for the client and for ourselves. We don't need discomfort or "weird vibes" interfering with our work as spiritual healers.

The next boundary we need to maintain involves not discussing our personal problems with our clients. They come to us for help and support — not to provide us with support. They don't come to listen to us. I'm guilty of crossing this boundary from time to time myself. There are some clients I have developed close relationships with. In fact, some clients who have serious problems come to see me every week. We build up trust with each other, and often we seem to have a lot in common. One day she or he comes for the appointment, and I'm having a bad day or something happened to me. As soon as they ask how I am, I tell them everything. This changes the whole relationship and dynamic. When she or he is helping me to heal, the boundaries get all fuzzy. With the client listening to and focusing on *my* problems, roles are confused and boundaries blurred.

You may think that crossing this line once or twice is no big deal, but once this boundary is broached, it's hard to go back. Trust me. I've learned the hard way. There are times when you may share parts of your life experience with a client to let them know you've been through a situation similar to theirs. That's different. When you share a life experience, you're being empathic. When you ask a client to listen to your problems, you've reversed your professional roles.

The next boundary we need to stay clear on is protecting our clients' confidentiality. Clients need to feel safe opening up to you. Perhaps the person is well known, and while it may give us a thrill to tell others that we've done a healing on "so-and-so," we fail our client if we do so. It is not enough to create a safe space in our offices. We must also provide the safety and security of our discretion between visits.

Last but not least, we need to remember that unless we are trained to give professional psychological advice, we cannot act as therapists. That's called practicing medicine without a license, and it is both ethically and legally wrong. We are channels for healing. If you are a trained therapist and are channeling healings as well, that's fine. But if you are a channel for healing and are not trained to professionally handle people's emotional or mental problems, just channel healing to them and, if it seems appropriate, refer them to someone reputable in your community for additional counseling.

Some people falsely believe that if we channel healing energy, we are right up there with God. Unfortunately, some clients want to invest us with this kind of power and authority. Even more unfortunately, some healers work to give their clients this impression. We are not authorities on healing; we are not doctors or God. We are channels for healing, and we need to keep it that simple.

I'd like to review the boundaries covered in this chapter:

- Create an atmosphere where clients feel safe enough to do their emotional work.

- Your touch needs to be firm enough to create a feeling of safety, but not intrusive or hurtful in any way.

- We cannot be sexual with our clients in any way.

- Open communication is very important.

- We need to be clear with ourselves as to what feels right and what doesn't feel right for us.

- We don't need to touch the affected area in order to bring about a healing.

- We should not discuss our personal problems with our clients.

- We need to protect the client's confidentiality.

- Unless we are trained professionals, we cannot get into advising our clients. Leave that to the experts!

- We have to always remember that we are not an authority on what our client needs. We cannot play doctor or God. We channel the healing and empower our client to listen to their own inner voice as to what they need in order to heal.

Chapter 6

Dependency / Crushes

Once in a while you may find one of your clients becoming dependent on you. I have had some people throughout the years tell me they didn't want to be completely healed because then they couldn't keep coming for healings. They love receiving the nurturing they feel from being touched. For some people, receiving laying-on-hands healing is the only time they are touched in a loving or nonsexual way.

This has always been a difficult situation for me to deal with. I had to tell one client that I would not channel any more healings to her — and it was very difficult for me to say that. She was a woman in her middle thirties. She was a therapist. Her job was very stressful. She didn't know how to get her own needs met in a healthy way. Her way of getting love was by getting sick. She would get a lot of attention from her husband and friends every time she got an illness. By the time she first came to me for healings, she had had over a dozen operations. It took me a while to see what was going on, but one evening I finally understood.

This client had been coming for healing of a lump in her arm that her doctors felt should be surgically removed. The lump disappeared after a few healings, but then she called to say that her doctors had told her she was going blind. That night while I was working on her eyes, I checked out clairvoyantly what was happening to her body. I saw pictures of a past life where she had been crippled. She had a lot of nurturing and a lot of love in that lifetime. I saw sadness inside of her soul because she missed the nurturing, the touching, the love. Subconsciously, the only way she knew how to get what she needed physically and emotionally was to be sick.

I told her about the images I had seen after I finished the healing. She told me that asking the people in her life to give her what she needed from them emotionally terrified her. She said the only way she ever got any attention from her mother was when she was sick. My guides suggested that she give a lot of thought to finding new and healthy ways to get the love and attention she was needing so badly.

We did a few more healings on her eyes, and the problem cleared up. About a month later, she wanted to come for healings on her legs because they were getting arthritic. After her legs were healed, she called for healings on her breasts. She told me she had had surgery on them and needed to get healed from the surgery in order to get back to work.

The whole situation felt uncomfortable to me. I felt bad for her, and really concerned for her body. I had a long talk with her one night. I told her that it was time to stop putting her body through all of this and that she had to start finding healthy ways of getting her emotional needs met, now. I told her I wasn't gong to channel anymore healings to her. I felt like I had become one of the enablers in her life.

At the time I didn't know if what I did was right or wrong, but it felt right to do. I talked to her about two months later, and she told me she was doing very well physically and that she was back in therapy herself. She said she was finding ways to get the love and nurturing she needed — other than getting sick.

When a client has made some comment about not wanting to be completely healed because they want to continue coming for healings, I tell them that their attitude has a lot to do with the healing process and that they could possibly be blocking the healing. I turn the conversation to other ways they can get nurturing, and I continue to focus on "life after illness" until they no longer come for healings.

You can also tell them they can continue to receive healings periodically to maintain good health, but the first thing is to get them healed.

There are better ways to get love and nurturing than being sick. If you suspect that your client is someone who uses illness as a way to receive nurturing, encourage them to find other, healthy ways.

Crushes

ANOTHER ISSUE, especially for male healers, is that your clients may develop a crush on you. I say male healers more so than female healers because a lot of women don't have someone in their life who is nurturing, gentle, and caring about their health. When a client comes for a healing and receives those things from the healer, some misinterpret that to mean that the healer loves them in an "in love with them" sort of way.

We need to maintain professional boundaries at all times. You need to find a way to be loving and caring, without being *too* loving and caring.

Chapter 7

Watch That Ego

One of the things we have to always remember is that we are channels for the healing energy. God is the Healer. The energy that flows through us as channels is God's healing energy, not ours.

My ego feels wonderful when I hear someone say, "Echo healed me." I feel important. I feel needed. But I have found that I can't allow myself the luxury of feeling things like that. I need to always remember who the Healer is and who the channel is. The day I start to believe that I am the one with the power, I'm in big trouble!

Let me explain what I mean by "big trouble." Being on the spiritual path I chose, I believe God is my source for everything. I ask God's guidance in all my affairs, whether it is my work, my home, finances, my relationships, my health, or my shortcomings.

I lived a fair number of years without a close, trusting relationship with God. My life was pure self-will — running riot. The difference between believing I was running the show and relying on God for His inner guidance is enormous.

Before getting on a "spiritual path," I was a practicing alcoholic. I believed I ran the show. I was full of self-doubt. I had a lot of self-destructive behavior. I was too proud to reach out for help or admit to myself that I needed help. I made decisions about my life based on fear, anger, loneliness, resentments, and low self-worth.

❖

"If we are going to take the credit when they heal, then we need to take responsibility if they don't heal."
— John

❖

I had a false sense of ego in the sense of not wanting anyone to know who or what I really was. I'd project the image of someone who really had her life in order. I tried to project confidence and happiness, yet the whole time I was terrified because I felt so alone, so unhappy.

I tried controlling outcomes. I felt responsible for other people's happiness. I wasn't doing a very good job of taking care of myself, so I tried taking care of everyone else's life. I felt I knew what other people needed (self-will), and I would do whatever I could to get it for them, or to make them change. Before I came to believe in a Higher Power, I didn't know what a "flow" was.

After I joined a recovery program for alcoholics, I began to develop a personal relationship with my Higher Power. The program taught me God would restore me and my life if I gave Him a chance. Over the years, I have come to rely on this power greater than myself to guide me in my daily life and with all my affairs. Living without Divine Guidance is going backward for me. It's empty. It's scary. Living with full acceptance of God is beautiful. It's flowing. It's harmonious.

So, when I say I'm in big trouble when I start believing I am the one with the power, I don't mean I'm in trouble with God, or with my family, or with the law. I am in big trouble with myself in the sense that I am where I don't want to be!

Here is another example of getting our ego out of joint and giving our power away.

Several years ago I had an experience with a doctor who came for a spiritual healing. I would like to share this story with you so that you don't get caught up in the same situation.

The first time he came for a healing I was very intimidated. I felt like I had to prove that healing works. Then, he asked all kinds of medical questions, making my sense of intimidation even worse. I felt we were speaking different languages. (We were!) He told me he did not want me to write his real name in my appointment book, just in case one of his patients came to me and happened to look in the book. He always wanted me to schedule enough time out so that he would be gone before my next client arrived. I gave this man a lot of power. I went along with his paranoia because I really wanted to show him that healing worked. He always wanted explanations in detail of what was happening during a healing. He was getting better — but would always find a logical, rational reason for why that was so (for example, medication he was on). It was very difficult for him to acknowledge that healing energy actually worked.

One day it occurred to me that we were in an "ego battle," and I was just as much at fault for what was going on as he was. I had a serious talk with him about my feelings. I told him I could not explain spiritual healing in standard medical terms. I told him I was intimidated by him because he was a doctor and that I needed to change my attitude and think of him as a person and not a doctor. I stopped feeling so defensive about myself and what I was doing. I took my power back. Shortly after this, he stopped coming for healings.

If you find yourself in a similar situation, I caution you about giving your power away. Don't feel apologetic. Don't feel you need to prove anything. How can we explain a spiritual experience intellectually? It is not entirely possible. Something gets lost in the translation, so just leave it alone. If a client is having a difficult time understanding this, suggest to them that they pray for an understanding. They will get their answers if they do that.

I don't want you to get the impression that all physicians are like this man. Many are open to spiritual healing. I tell you the above story so that you don't get caught up in an ego battle with someone in the medical field, or, for that matter, any other field.

Power

THERE ARE TWO other important areas concerning power that I would like to address: misusing our power and giving our power away.

Recently I had a woman come for a healing who had been traumatized by a male healer. He had told her that in order for healing to be effective, she needed to remove all of her clothes. This woman had had severe pain for quite a while and had become discouraged with the medical profession. She told me that when she visited the male healer she was at the point at which she would have done anything to get rid of her pain. She also said that because this man was a healer, she assumed he was on a spiritual path and therefore wouldn't do anything that was wrong. So in spite of her instincts and intuition, which were telling her not to do it, she went ahead and removed her clothing. At the end of her session this healer kissed her, telling her it was part of the healing ceremony!

After a few of these sessions, my client and the male healer became sexual. She told me that at each successive visit, the healer became more sexually aggressive with her, telling her it was part of the healing.

Physically she was feeling better, but she was feeling a lot of confusion and shame about what was happening. This healer was married. He of course told her not to discuss their sessions with others. She later found out he was doing this with another woman. She came to me for healing for the shame and to get clarity on what was real and what wasn't. I remember her looking at me so naively and saying, "I thought all healers were on a spiritual path. How could this have happened?"

This story illustrates both misusing power and giving power away. When people come to us for healing, they often feel that we are their last hope. They are vulnerable and we cannot take advantage of that. We need to be sympathetic to their vulnerability and help empower them, not take their power away and make them feel worse. We need to be responsible and professional and have integrity in our work.

The other part to this story is that my client gave all of her power away to the male healer she consulted. She said everything inside told her not to take her clothes off; she knew it didn't feel right, but she honored him because he was a healer — and didn't honor herself.

My psychic teacher was a controlling woman. When I first began taking classes from her, I gave her a lot of power. She was, after all, the teacher, and had had years and years of experience. Who was I to question her? I did whatever she told me to do. As I started getting a stronger self-worth and listening to my own inner voice, rather than her voice, I stopped giving her so much power. She didn't like this because in the past she'd been able to control me just by giving me one of her "looks."

We finally had a showdown, and I took my power back. I had found my own inner guide and had to listen to and live by that, rather than to how this teacher wanted me to live or think or be. Empowerment has been one of my issues this lifetime, not giving others more credit than I give to myself. Believing others are smarter or more creative or more loving or more of whatever. Perhaps that's why stories like my client's really push my buttons. It's hard to discern, when we're down and out, who's telling the truth, which health-care practitioner is the one with integrity and which one is a sex addict. But we need to learn to discern. We need to listen to our own inner voice of intuition, and when it says to get as far away from this person as you can, we need to listen to it and ask the Universe to direct us to the right person.

No matter what situation it is, whether you're listening to a medical doctor tell you that you need surgery or a psychic giving you advice, a well-known lecturer teaching something that feels weird or your mother telling you to buy the blue coat instead of the green one, we have to empower ourselves to listen to our own inner voice and learn discernment. If someone or something does not feel right, trust yourself and get yourself out of the situation. Don't give your power away.

To those who are thinking of becoming a healer because you like the idea of having power, why don't you work on empowering yourself instead of hoping others will. People trust us, and there is a tremendous responsibility with that trust. Don't traumatize someone because you have a need to feel power.

Chapter 8

First Things First

I would like to share with you another phase I went through as a spiritual healer, with the hope that you can avoid it.

It was 1978. I was a barber, working full time during the day. When there was a need, I would channel healings in the evening. I never advertised myself as a spiritual healer, but the word was spreading fast. I was getting a lot of calls from people with physical problems. My life was getting way out of balance.

At that point, I hadn't established any boundaries for myself. I felt such a strong sense of responsibility to anyone who needed a healing.

Mentally, I was feeling scattered. Physically, I was getting run down. I would drink a lot of caffeine and eat a lot of sugar to keep up this pace.

I assumed that because I had this gift, this was how I was to live my life. I had no social life. No play time. No routine for myself.

I was getting to the point where I was feeling resentful about my gift. It felt more like a burden. The sense of responsibility I felt was driving me crazy! I was feeling resentful, which then I'd feel guilty about.

I don't remember how long this went on, but I do remember clearly what stopped all of it. I went through a three-day period of being very sick, followed by a two-week stay in the hospital, which included surgery on my colon. I was completely run down and so confused. I was also angry with God. I had this idea in my head that as long as I was doing God's work, He would take care of me, so why was I in the hospital?

Clients were calling me at the hospital. Some were very upset with me. "How could I be sick?" they'd ask. I was a healer. I wasn't supposed to get sick. They had forgotten I was a human being — more importantly, I had forgotten.

It hadn't occurred to me that the first responsibility I had was to myself.

It wasn't God's fault that I was in the hospital. It turned out to be a blessing in disguise, because I was forced to stop the way of life I had created and take a look at it.

I was never very good at being assertive and saying no. Setting boundaries for myself was very scary, and yet I knew it was essential for my health and well-being that I do so. I had to learn about a balanced way of life. Working, eating properly, getting eight hours of sleep every night, finding time to play, to be creative, to have a social life, to be alone, to keep up with my financial responsibilities, and staying on a spiritual path so that I was getting spiritually filled up — all these things needed a place in my life. In neglecting to keep these things balanced, I had overlooked a tremendous responsibility to myself.... I had to get back on track.

Making Room for What's Important

I HAD A FRIEND make a healing table for me, and I began to have my clients come to my home for their healings instead of me driving to them.

I wish you could have seen my first healing table. It was great! It was made with an old metal ladder, some plywood, and some foam rubber. It was very comfortable. I was so proud of it. My friend made it high enough off the floor so I could either sit or stand comfortably for as long as needed. I sit during most of the healings that I channel, so it's important to have the table at a comfortable height for my arms.

At first I worried about asking the clients to come to my home, but no one objected. If a person cannot get there, I will go to them, but very seldom is that the case. Now I have a portable healing table that I can take with me if necessary. It is important when you are channeling energy that you're comfortable, too. It's hard on your neck and back and legs when you have to crouch down for long periods of time.

Next, I had to set up a consistent schedule for the nights I would do healings and the nights I was free to do what I needed to do to keep some balance and order in my life. The difficult part was sticking to the schedule, saying to a client who had an urgent healing need that I had plans. My sense of responsibility would stab me with guilt pangs.

If someone calls now, I make an appointment to see them and then send an absentee healing in the meantime.

One very important thing for you and your clients to remember is that you are only human. You are the channel. Your client can ask

God for a healing. You do not need to be present in order for the healing to work (see Absentee Healings in chapter 1).

I had to develop a certain "detachment" about illness. We are surrounded by human beings with physical problems. We can tell people we channel healing energy but leave the responsibility of getting the healing up to them.

Find Your Own "Rules"

I DON'T FEEL comfortable saying to you, "Do this," or "Don't do that." It is important for you to find what's right for you.

I do feel comfortable asking you to be aware of the responsibility you have to yourself, however. Give some thought to boundaries. Be okay with your limitations. Give yourself permission to do what works for you.

I recently channeled a healing to a very sweet young man in his early twenties, who feels very strongly that his path this lifetime is to be a healer.

You are a channel for healing. You are a child of God. The better you take care of you — the better you'll be able to channel the beautiful, loving, healing energy.

He came for healing for a serious breathing problem and told me in our initial visit that he was in the process of getting rid of his ego. He worries that his ego is getting in the way of his being a healer.

After I was channeling healing to him for about five minutes, his spirit guide came to me and said, "Tell him to lighten up. He's gotten way too serious for such a young man. We don't want him to destroy his ego. His 'self.'" The guide said, "We rather like his ego; it's just that he's gotten too serious. Someone must tell him to lighten up. He must laugh and play again."

The guide went on to say that yes, this young man did come to this plane to be a healer, but that in order to be a teacher and a healer, he needed to live a more balanced life.

The guide also said that the young man's lungs weren't ready to heal, because the journey of getting his lungs healed would be his greatest teacher. He needed to learn discernment by seeing that many health-care practitioners are charlatans, while others are good. He needed not to be angry with his lungs for being imperfect, but to thank the condition because it was going to take him where he wanted to go.

The guide said to him, "If we were to leave you with any words of instruction for your journey as a healer, we would tell you to take a year, play hard, and laugh harder. Get back to the joy in life and stop frowning."

I wasn't certain how the young man was going to take this information because he had said nothing during the healing. My hands could feel his body blocking the healing. During the healing I told him to visualize a zipper in the area of his lungs and to visualize unzipping it to let in more healing. But his lungs said no to my hands, that their condition served a purpose and to just let the man be with it.

I left the room for about five minutes and came back. The young man was sitting on the end of the healing table with a huge smile on his face. He said, "You have no idea how stuffy I have become," and then he hugged me really hard and thanked me over and over for liberating him. He told me that he had spiritual disciplines that he made himself do every day and that he had become extremely serious about everything. He told me he couldn't remember the last time he laughed.

When he left, he promised he would relearn how to play, how to laugh, and how to have a balanced life.

An Update

SINCE WRITING THIS back in 1983, my body has been through many changes because of being a channel for healing energy.

Every so often, and there is no set timing on this, my body goes through a process to take me to another level so that I can channel stronger energy.

The signs are not always the same, so sometimes I don't know I'm in one of these transitions until it passes and I begin channeling stronger energy.

These are the different changes I go through when my body is going to another level as a healer:

- Metallic taste in my mouth.

- My appetite increases quite a bit.

- I put on 5 to 10 pounds.

- I crave chocolate, baked potatoes, red meat, and coffee (decaf), and I drink gallons of water.

- I either stay up until two o'clock or three o'clock in the morning reading everything spiritual I can get my hands on, or I feel extremely creative and redecorate, sew, or write, OR I become extremely tired and sleep all the time.

- I become quite a hermit, hiding out from everyone including close friends and family members since it feels like I need to be in the "silence."

- I usually stop all physical activity such as running on my treadmill or going for walks.

- I get spacey and absentminded.

- I have dreams where I'm in a classroom learning something new.

- My body feels like it's going through a metamorphosis, like I'm in a cocoon and will soon emerge a butterfly.

- My hands start channeling stronger energy, and they can hurt, go numb, feel arthritic, or feel really fat and thick. They are very sensitive and don't like to be touched.

- Sometimes when I go through these periods, I don't want anyone to touch me or hug me.

- I feel like I'm in some kind of chamber, and I don't want anyone "messing" with my energy.

- Sometimes I can hear voices far away teaching me something, yet my conscious mind can't make them out; they sound muddled.

These periods last seven to ten days, and when I come out of them, I go back to normal, except I know I've come through something really important and am now a stronger channel. My diet goes back to normal. I get off coffee and cut way back on the sugar, the red meat, and the chocolate. I lose the weight I put on. My mind becomes more clear, and I'm less forgetful. I naturally crave fun, movies, people, and socializing in place of the solitude I craved before.

I go for months or maybe a year before I go into one of these changes, but seem to go through at least one of these transitions every year.

I asked my guide why I've been going through so many of them lately after all these years. He told me it was because I am getting better at "hearing" my body and what she needs. He told me it is important that I am as connected to my body as I am, because my body does require certain things if I am going to be a healer.

Shortly after that conversation with my guide, I saw my holistic MD for a checkup on my thyroid, which was a little slow. He asked me how much medication I was taking, and I told him that each day I asked my body how much she wanted for the day and that that's how much I took, which ran between three and four tablets each morning. He said that it was great that I could do that because not many people could, and when he said that, I understood what my guide had meant. Up until the doctor said that, I wasn't sure what my guide meant because I thought hearing the body was something everyone did!

I have learned to honor my body. If she needs a massage, I get one. A good soak in the tub? A run on the treadmill? Maybe get outdoors and do some yard work to get more grounded? Total quiet? No phones, music, TV? Silence? I listen to her. I "feel" when she needs supplements such as magnesium, calcium, chromium, liver support, vitamin B, and an extra thyroid tablet or hormone tablet. I ask her what she needs, and I can feel her need. Sometimes she needs a visit to the chiropractor or dinner with a nurturing friend. My inner child may need to cuddle with one of my stuffed animals. No, it's not what my head says; it's what my body says.

It's taken me quite a few years to get to the point where I can hear what my body is saying. I always used to eat what my taste buds wanted. I dressed the way I thought I "should." I took supplements according to the doctor's orders. I went on diets because others wanted me to. I did a lot of things according to what others wanted or needed me to do, but over the years, that has changed.

I think a lot of it changed because of all that I learned about my body through working with my chiropractor and kinesiology. Also because of my own work with the healings, I've seen how individualized we all are.

It's very important, if you are going to be on the path of a spiritual healer, to be able to hear what your body is saying. Each body has very specific needs and wants. Let me give you a quick example: Do you crave chocolate? Well, did you know that chocolate has magnesium in it? The next time you have a chocolate craving, try taking a magnesium supplement instead. Magnesium is very calming. It helps us sleep better, among other things. I didn't know that. I just knew that each night before I went to bed, I craved chocolate. I told my doctor I craved chocolate every night, and he told me to take magnesium instead, which I now do. The point is that if our bodies need something, they will crave it in one form or another. Before you get too judgmental with yourself, check out what's in the thing you're craving and take that instead!

Life-changing Healings

IN AUGUST 1992, I went through one of the most difficult transitions I had ever experienced. I had all the symptoms and was very emotional.

It took about one month to get through it. Until I did, my hands ached terribly on the days I did healings. Some nights I would wrap them in a heating pad just to help ease the pain.

My guide at that time was named David. He came to me one night when I was feeling really confused because I couldn't tell what was happening. He told me I was going to a higher level as a healer than I had ever been and would soon start channeling life-changing healings. He told me my client load would change very soon because many of the people who were coming at that time for healings wouldn't be able to handle this stronger healing energy. He said the universe would only send clients to me who could handle this new energy.

At first I didn't believe David because the clients I had were coming weekly and had been for some time. But sure enough, about two days after he gave me that information, almost every client stopped coming, one by one. Most of them said it just felt like they needed to take a break, that they were going to try something else, or that because of finances they were going to wait a while.

David told me I would no longer be able to channel six healings a day. I was only to do four maximum per day.

Normally, my office would receive several calls per week, and what happened was amazing for me to watch. The phone literally stopped ringing for about two weeks while I continued to go through this transformation, and then one or two calls would come in. Completely different clients called. When these new people would come, their healings were unbelievable — very strong and longer than usual. The healing energy seemed to take them into a very deep process of healing. I loved being part of what was happening, but financially, it was awful! I dropped down from six healings a day to one. When I would pray for understanding or ask David to help me understand what was happening, he told me I would continue to go to higher levels as a channel for healing, but I needed to be really patient and trusting with the process. The intention was to take me to higher and higher places and therefore take my clients to higher places in their healing process. He told me I needed to be willing to make any changes in my life that were necessary and not to hang on to everything as it was. I should not fight the change and would be really happy when I was through it, but in the meantime, I needed to trust God that everything was going to be okay financially.

What was happening with my clients was wonderful. Right after the change began, I channeled a healing to a woman who had suffered from depression all of her life. I channeled an incredibly strong healing to her, and she left saying she'd call when she felt it was time to come back. Two months later I ran into her at church. She said she had not suffered any depression since that day at my office!

I ran into another woman at the grocery store who told me she had had no more back pain since she came for her one healing.

I started hearing this from others who had come only once.

I felt really blessed to be a part of all of this. I had always wanted to channel this kind of energy, but going through the transformation was very difficult.

Financially it was devastating, and that lasted for about three months. It was a very slow process of getting used to the new energy. I slept a lot. I prayed a lot. And some days, I cried a lot. At times I wondered if I was to get out of the healing business altogether, because the calls were so slow in coming. But looking back now, I realize that I could really only handle channeling a very few of those healings at first. I'm glad I stuck it out and didn't go get a job, as I was tempted to do so many days when the bill collectors were calling and no clients were. As hard as it was to go through, I gained an inner strength that I will always have, and I don't know if I could have gotten it in any other way.

It was a truly transforming time for me in many ways. My life seemed to shift over to a very positive place, and it has continued to stay positive.

Clients are coming again, but the healings and the clients are very different. They continue to be very intense, and sessions last quite a bit longer than before. They used to be twenty to thirty minutes long; now they are forty-five to sixty minutes long. The clients that are coming are open to going very deep in their process. There's a "let's go for it" attitude in the people I'm seeing. Most are in or have been in therapy and have done a lot of their emotional work so that their healing is ready to come together.

Not all of the people coming in right now are ready to receive this new energy, and I can feel the energy trying to be moderate with them. The flow of energy is gentler, almost as if my hands have to hold back. But the nicest part of this for me is that God is in control of each of the healings, and I don't have to figure out who is ready for this energy and who needs a little less. The Universe is on top of the situation!

I should also say not everyone is experiencing instantaneous healings. As I have said in just about every chapter in this book, people get healed when they are ready. And they will be led to the right healer at the right time.

Our job as healers, besides listening to what others need, is to learn to listen to what our body needs and wants. Be sure to keep a balance in your life and honor yourself above all else. You will do some incredible work as a channel for healing. Stay clear on your priorities and keep first things first.

Chapter 9

Money

The area that seems to bring up the most anguish for people in spiritual healing is whether or not to take money or charge money for healing.

Several years ago, when I started channeling healing to people other than my family, I didn't know what I should do about charging money for healings. I was afraid if I charged money or took donations, God would get mad at me for being materialistic and take my gift away. Fortunately for me, I was working full time as a barber during the day while I started my career as a healer. It was a good arrangement in the beginning, working during the day to support myself and doing healings at night. After a few months, however, my energy was running low, and my arms ached from working as a barber. I knew I had to make a decision to do one career or the other: be a barber or be a healer and psychic. I just did not have the energy to be good at both.

The decision was a very difficult one for me because as a barber, I had a secure, well-paying job and "fit into the real world." I could pick and choose who I wanted to know about my healing and psychic abilities. If I quit my secure barbering job and "came out of the closet" with my other abilities, everyone would know, and I didn't feel very comfortable being that vulnerable.

I prayed and meditated. I asked God daily for signs, clear signs as to what to do. Which path should I travel down? What would people think of me? Could I make it financially? How would I get enough business to have a busy, successful career? There was much fear and doubt.

After anguishing for about a month, I felt an inner guidance that it was time to quit barbering and follow my path, which was to be a psychic and spiritual healer. The one area I could not get peaceful with was whether or not to charge money for the healings.

I asked everyone I knew what they thought I should do. Everyone had a different opinion. One of my friends told me that if I started taking money for spiritual healing, he wouldn't be my friend anymore. He said it was wrong to mix money with spiritual gifts and that the healers in the Bible all had "day jobs" as tent makers, carpenters, et cetera.

I made a decision to charge money for psychic readings, but would not charge for healings until I was clearly shown what to do. While waiting for "my sign," I was slowly going into debt. I was making a fourth of the income I had been making as a barber, but I felt an inner determination to stay on my path and continue to wait for my sign from God. I clearly needed more money. I was getting increasingly stressed from all the financial pressures I had, but I had this terrible fear God would get mad at me for charging for the healing energy, which wasn't mine; it didn't come from me, just through me.

I continued to pray for clear guidance and continued to have financial problems. At one point, I sold all my furniture and moved out of my nice apartment into a furnished studio apartment. I applied for General Assistance, something I had never had to do before. They told me as long as I owned a car, they couldn't give me any assistance.

I felt so betrayed by God. I believed in my heart that if God really loved me, he would take care of me, but it didn't seem to be the case here. Something was really wrong, and I didn't know what to do.

It was a very difficult time, and looking back, I wonder where I got the gumption to keep going. Thank God I had my mom! There were many nights I ate dinner at her place and many times when she paid my rent and car payments.

One evening, I felt like I had hit bottom. I was yelling at God about abandoning me. Why did this way of life have to be so difficult? Why did I have to lose everything in order to do what I believed was His will in my life? I screamed at him that if he didn't give me some answers, I was going back to barbering. Even though I didn't think I could really do that, I felt desperate. The next morning an acquaintance called and asked if we could have breakfast. We met that morning. He told me that he was told in meditation to pay my rent for one year while I got on my feet financially. He asked me what was happening in my life. I told him how hard everything was, and he said he felt very sure this is what he was supposed to do. My mind was blown! The only condition was that he didn't want me to tell anyone he was doing this. You can probably imagine how this all felt — surprising, humbling, embarrassing. I felt very grateful to this man for listening to God and to God for listening to me.

The next thing that happened was that our local newspaper did a very nice article on me and my business took off. Clients were asking me if they could give me some money for the healings. They said they wanted to give back to me. I had bill collectors calling all the time, and I still didn't recognize "my sign." I didn't want to do anything wrong. It did feel like an important part of people's process was for them to give back, so I donated all the money I received from healings to a local charitable organization. That only lasted for a short time because some of the board members of the organization found out I was a psychic and asked me not to affiliate with them anymore. Once again I was faced with what to do with the money.

The newspaper article brought in a lot of business. I slowly started accepting the money, more out of desperation than from a feeling that I had been given a clear sign to do so. I charged $15.00 per session and half expected God to take my healing abilities away from me.

What I found though was that He never took them away. And as my financial problems began clearing up, I felt much less stressed and was able to be a more clear channel because I wasn't so distracted by financial worries.

It wasn't until the summer of 1980, almost two years after I quit barbering and became a full-time psychic and healer, that I got peaceful about taking money for healing. I finally got my "clear sign."

Alberto Aguas, an internationally known healer from Brazil, came to Minneapolis to do a three-evening workshop on healing. I had heard of this man for years but had never met him. The second night of the workshop, one of the participants asked Mr. Aguas how he "justified taking money for spiritual healing." Alberto looked at him and said very calmly, "Sir, there are two kinds of healers in the world. The kind that pay their bills and the kind that don't. I choose to be responsible and pay my bills. And besides that, I do not charge for the healing energy, I charge for my time." Praise the Lord and Hallelujah! I wanted to jump up on the tables and do an Irish jig. All I could think was finally...I got my sign. I'm charging for my time. Not for the healing energy. I wanted to grab this man and give him a big kiss for finally "setting me free." Over the years I have prayed for guidance as to when to raise my prices and what to raise them to. We need to keep our rates reasonable so that people can come often. Healing is usually a process. Very seldom is it a one-time visit. The other thing to take into consideration when setting your price is that people unfortunately often get to us after they've exhausted everything else, so there's a fine line between taking care of others and taking care of ourselves. If you are at a place in your healing practice where it feels time to start charging for your services, ask the Universe to help you know what the best price is at this time. It will change from time to time. Your intuition will let you know when it's time for a raise.

Chapter 10

Frequently Asked Questions

People are fascinated by spiritual healing and always have a lot of questions. This chapter will cover the questions most commonly asked. I will also share with you the answers I have found to be true for myself. I would strongly suggest that you look within yourself for your own answers, for you will find that you have your own individual responses that may differ in some respects from my responses. But my own answers may help you in finding your own, for when people find out you're a channel for healing energy, you will be asked a lot of these same questions.

Question: Are you drained after a healing?

Answer: Never. It's not my energy that I channel. What can be and is draining is working with people day after day. It's hard to hear all the pain and suffering people go through. That's why, like Jesus, we need to take lots of breaks from our work and keep everything in a healthy perspective.

Question: Is there any physical problem that can't be healed?

Answer: This question always strikes me as funny. The answer is no. I have never come up against anything that God can't heal! There isn't any problem that can't be healed. However, I do want to say something about an aspect of healing that I don't understand very well. A person can go to one healer and get no results, then go to another one, and be healed. Both healers could work in the same way — but one will have excellent results with the client, and the other one won't! So, don't be discouraged if a healing doesn't seem to be working. The healing may be happening at a soul level or maybe on the emotional level. It's hard not to judge the healing energy when we don't see physical results, but remember, something is always happening on some level. Maybe it's karmic that they receive their healing from someone else. There is another point to this as well: the client may have been receiving a heal-ing the whole time from the first healer, but the results came about at the time they went to the second healer. I have had clients whom I've sensed I was not going to be able to help. I refer them to other healers when I sense this. As I said, I don't understand this aspect of healing. I have heard other healers talk of it, too. Fortunately, since we are channels for healing, it isn't necessary that we understand everything in order for healing to take place, as long as we know what steps to take for the welfare of the client.

Question: If I'm sick, can I still channel energy?

Answer: I don't channel energy when I'm not feeling well, mainly because I don't want to give my client what I have. There have been times when I'm not sick, but when my own personal energy is low. Still, when I chan-nel healing, the healing energy is very strong, in spite of how I'm feeling.

Question: What if before or during a healing you feel tense or uptight? Will that block the healing and what do you do to relieve the tension?

Answer: No, my feeling tense will not block the energy. Usually as I am positioning myself in my chair, getting my body into a comfortable position, I take several deep breaths, blowing out any stress or tension I may be feeling, and I ask the Universe to please clear me (see section on clearing, page 4).

Likewise with a client, when they begin experiencing different emotions, i.e., sadness, anger, fear, et cetera, or become aware of feeling tense or blocked, I suggest to them that they take several deep breaths (from their abdomen) and breathe out — visualizing the word release.

❖

Releasing is a very important part
of the healing process.

❖

Release what? Any old emotions, memories, and physical and/or emotional pain. For example, if a client begins feeling a lot of sadness while I am channeling a healing to them, I tell them not to hang onto the sadness by intellectualizing it.

I suggest to clients that they go with the emotions: let it flow, cry it out if that's what their body needs to do, or talk it out and then either silently or verbally say, "I release you, I release you."

Question: Do you ever get the person's illness?

Answer: No, I have never picked up a person's illness or gotten physically sick myself from channeling healing energy. There have been times when I have felt a strange kind of pain in my hands while channeling a healing, but it disappears within an hour after starting. As far as where the illness goes, I don't know the "real" answer. I have always assumed the disease is dissolved by the healing energy.

Question: Do your hands always get hot during a healing?

Answer: No. There have been times I have felt no heat, but the client has. Sometimes it's the other way around. I've done some channeling when my hands feel like they're on fire, but the client feels nothing. Sometimes the energy coming through feels like a cool mentholatum.

Question: Is it necessary for the clients to take off their clothes?

Answer: I never ask a client to remove clothing. The healing energy flows through layers of anything.

Question: Since it's important that the person ask for the healing, is it okay to pray for a healing for someone if they don't know about it?

Answer: I can't imagine it not being okay to pray for anyone as long as I keep in mind "Thy will be done," not mine. But I would not channel an absentee healing without the person's knowledge and request for it, unless they were a child or were in a coma or unconscious and a family member had requested a healing. Then I would just ask God to please give so-and-so a healing according to their highest good.

Question: Is it all right to smoke during healing?

Answer: No, I don't believe the person channeling the healing or the person receiving a healing should smoke during a healing. I think the people involved (healer and "healee") should focus on the healing process rather than on smoking a cigarette.

Question: What music should I play while channeling a healing?

Answer: The problem with answering that question is that there are hundreds of wonderful recordings. Follow your intuition, and go to local bookstores for suggestions. Here are some artists whose work I like to use: Steven Halpern, Yanni, Kitaro, Aeoliah, Daniel Kobialka, Rusty Crutcher, David Parsons, and Paul Fitzgerald.

Question: Some people want to know how they can know for sure that it isn't Satan healing them.

Answer: I have read in Corinthians in the Bible that of all the Gifts of the Spirit, the only one Satan doesn't have is the gift of healing. Only God has the power to heal, and that's what I tell clients.

Question: Have you ever done a healing on an animal?

Answer: Yes, and plants too!

Question: Is it okay to use a healing table with metal in it?

Answer: Yes. Some books may tell you it's not okay. Some may say you have to use a wooden table. Some may say you have to meditate for an hour every day or fast for two out of every seven days. Another book might say you have to use oil. Some say to stand in a south-north direction, or not to stand on cement, or not to let the client wear jewelry or digital watches, to light white candles, et cetera. For a while, I was getting all caught up in these kinds of do's and don'ts, but I have to say that whether I'm following them or not, the healing energy always comes through.

Question: How do you handle skeptics?

Answer: I used to feel I needed to defend healing, but not anymore. I believe everyone is entitled to their opinion. I listen to their beliefs, but I don't get into debates as I did sometimes in the past. I no longer try to convince people that healing works. The healing energy speaks for itself.

Question: Does laying-on-hands healing heal emotional problems or addictions, such as alcoholism?

Answer: Addictions such as alcoholism entail more than physical problems. I believe a person suffering from any kind of major addiction is suffering physical, mental, emotional, and spiritual bankruptcy, and in order to receive total healing, each of these areas must be addressed. I am not a trained therapist and would not limit the client's chances to recover by pretending to be one. If a person is emotionally or mentally ill, I refer them to someone qualified to help them with that.

Question: Can I heal myself?

Answer: This question can be answered in two ways:

1. When I have been in physical pain, I have asked God to please do a healing on the problem, and I have always received the healing. I'll never forget the day I came home from the hospital after having a hysterectomy. My stomach had a 12-inch scar on it, and I was sore. I lay on my bed, placed my hands on my body, and asked God to please do a healing on me because I had a lot of things to do and didn't want to go through the usual six-week recuperation period. I felt a deep heat through my entire body. I fell asleep. I woke up about an hour later feeling like a brand-new person. The next day I went shopping. I was back to work in only three weeks. Receiving a healing

is a wonderful experience. It's hard to describe the sense of nurturing. The loving energy is so "filling up."

2. I ask my body what the illness is trying to tell me. I am as open as possible to truly hearing, seeing or feeling what is going on inside. The more willing I am to face any emotions I may need to deal with, the easier self-healing is.

When I feel a need for a healing, I lie on my healing table, play some relaxing music, ask the Universe to clear me, body, mind, and soul, lay my hands on my solar plexus, and ask God to channel healing through me. It works!

Self-healing involves honesty with yourself, above all else. You need to be willing to open yourself up to your own self, as completely as possible. Be willing to hear, see, or feel what's really going on.

Question: Should a client discontinue medication while receiving healing?

Answer: No. Do not tell anyone to get off medication while getting healings. That is called practicing medicine without a license, and we can be thrown in jail for it. We are not even (legally) allowed to tell people to take vitamins. Just stick to the healings.

Question: Should a person forego medical help or surgery and just get healings?

Answer: I would never tell a client not to see a doctor or not to have surgery. Doctors and medicine can be another avenue for healing. Some people are under the impression that healers and doctors are at war with each other, and even though in some cases that may be true, I think that in general, most healers are respectful of doctors and medicine.

Question: How often can a person receive a healing?

Answer: Daily and maybe even twice a day. You need to listen to their body and your intuition to know how much and how often they can handle getting healings.

Question: How does a person know when they're ready to be a full-time healer?

Answer: My psychic teacher told me it takes at least twenty years of practice before a person is truly ready to be a full-fledged healer or psychic. She said there were numerous situations and experiences that we needed to have before we could call ourselves ready.

I do not tell my students they need to practice for twenty years, but I do try to stress the importance of not being in a hurry. There is so much to learn and ninety percent of it comes through the experiences you will have while practicing on family members and friends. The answer varies with each person. I have to go back to my standard answer, which is to go within and ask God to show you when you're ready. I would recommend getting some experience — how to handle clients who get emotional, how to handle life/death situations, what your beliefs are, how to deal with skeptics/family members/medical people, channeling different kinds of healings, et cetera.

Being a spiritual healer takes a lot of dedication. It calls for a well-developed relationship with God because this is teamwork. We need to be able to communicate with the other half of our team if we're going to be successful.

Many different situations are going to come up and we need to be able to hear God (our intuition) guide us.

I can usually tell which students are going to be successful and which ones will fizzle out after a while.

The successful ones are the students who have a humility about this work. They take their time, are in awe of the power of the energy, have a "why me?" attitude, and develop a strong relationship with God. The unsuccessful dive in, feeling they are ready right away and getting into this work to become wealthy or because they can't find anything else to do. The people who aren't willing to go through the different learning phases usually fizzle out after a while because they become disillusioned. They thought it was going to be glamorous to be thought of as a healer.

This is a career that develops slowly. It takes time to build up an inner and an outer confidence in the energy and in yourself as a channel.

How long does it take? Every person is different. Here are my suggestions:

- Don't be in a hurry.

- Establish a good working relationship with God (your intuition).

- Practice on friends and family members as often as you can.

- Don't quit your day job until you feel an inner calling from God that you're ready to do this.

- Don't focus on the day when you can charge money or do this full time as a career. Learn from each experience. It's the journey that's important, not the destination. If you are meant to be a spiritual healer, the day will come when it's time to do it. Don't push the river upstream.

Question: Do your hands suffer from doing this work?

Answer: Once when I was getting a massage, I noticed how sore my forearms were. My masseuse told me it was because healers often store healing energy in their forearms. She told me to get in the habit of rubbing my arms when I was sitting around relaxing at the end of the day. It does help my arms to feel better. Warm packs also help relieve the pain, and asking the Universe to please clear my arms of any energy I may have picked up helps a great deal as well. Sometimes when my hands feel "fat" or "full" from the energy, I'll dangle my arms to the side and gently shake them, asking the Universe to please clear them.

Chapter 11

Healing Is a Process

A common myth with spiritual healing is that when healers lay their hands on people with physical problems, those people are instantly healed. I will say that this is true in some cases, but more often than not a person goes through some kind of a transition between their first and last healing session.

In this chapter of case studies, I will devote a small portion to healings that were instantaneous, but the larger portion, as is usually the case, will be about different processes I have seen people go through to become healed.

Mary

A WOMAN OF fifty who went into the hospital for a hysterectomy. She had been told by her doctors that her recovery time would be longer because of her age, and that she could plan on being in the hospital for at least ten days and possibly two weeks. She asked me to please come in and do a healing on her when she came out of the recovery room, which I did.

I remember thinking how pale she looked. I was sure she was going to need more than just one healing, so I did a healing on her and left the hospital with that in mind. I called the hospital that night to see how she was doing, and they said she'd been resting comfortably ever since she had come back from surgery. The next morning I called her room about 8:00, but there was no answer. I panicked. My human, doubtful mind was thinking all kinds of negative thoughts. I called the nurses' station to find out what happened to her, and they said she'd been up walking around since 7:00 and doing just fine. She went home three days later!

Jonathan

JONATHAN WAS SEVEN. For years he had recurring herpes of the mouth and chin. He was also having trouble sleeping. His mother had taken him to several doctors, but nothing was working. The herpes would come and go at random. There didn't seem to be any specific pattern.

I placed a white handkerchief on his lips and chin and did a healing. He slept hard for almost one hour. When he awoke, the herpes was still there. His mother called the next day to say the herpes was gone.

During the healing, I was told by Jonathan's guides that every night when he went to bed he needed to listen to some very calming music. The guides told me Jonathan was psychically very sensitive and would "pick up" all kinds of things throughout a day. This made him very hyper by bedtime. I gave her a list of tapes that I use during healing (see suggestions on page 89).

I spoke with his mother several months later, and she told me that Jonathan was very faithful about listening to meditation-type music tapes every night at bedtime and that the herpes had never recurred after that one healing.

Arleen

ARLEEN HAD A STAPH INFECTION in her eyes. Both eyes were beet red, very full of pus, and very swollen. She had gone to an eye specialist who told her the infection was so bad that he was concerned she might

lose the sight in one of her eyes. He gave her some medication and told her to come back every day until it cleared up.

She called me that night, and I went over to her home. I had never seen anything like it. Her eyes were a mess. Any light was very painful, so she kept her sunglasses on. I had her sit in a chair. I put a white handkerchief and my left hand on the back of her head. The energy started flowing immedi-

I felt led to have Arleen sit in a chair in case her eyes drained during the healing, which they did.

ately. The eyes were draining like nobody's business! She was busy with tissues while I was praying for the healing. My right hand would fill up with a sharp pain, and then it would leave. Fill up and leave. Fill up and leave. This went on for about fifteen minutes. After about twenty minutes of healing, the energy stopped.

I was just about to ask her if she wanted me to come back the next day, when my inner voice told me it wouldn't be necessary. I did ask her if she would call me and let me know how she was doing. She called me the next afternoon after she had come home from the doctor's. She said the doctor was totally amazed at how her eyes had improved. She said he even called in one of the nurses to show how well Arleen was doing. Arleen was amazed. The infection was almost gone. The draining had stopped and the redness had cleared up. Once again, my inner voice knew what it was talking about!

Ted and His Back

ONE NIGHT I had a date with a man who understood very little about what I do professionally. He was about fifteen minutes late. When he got to my home, he was moving very slowly, and it was obvious he was in a lot of pain. He said he had pulled something in his back that afternoon while playing racquetball. I told him I could do a healing on his back if he wanted, but he was noticeably uncomfortable at the suggestion. He said we were late and that we'd better get going. We were due at a dinner party in ten minutes, so we left. But, on the way there, he asked me what "this healing stuff" was all about. I explained as much as I could in the limited time, but as we talked, my right hand began to heat up, and I could feel that it was "full" of energy. Even though he asked me questions, I could sense there was a part of him that didn't want to hear the answers.

As we walked up the stairs to our friends' house, Ted made the comment that maybe if the evening didn't get too late, I could do "one of those healings" on him. My right hand went right to the spot in his back that was in pain, and a huge bolt of energy came out of my hand. The energy was so intense it actually knocked him forward about a foot. He said, "What the hell was that!?" And I told him that was the healing energy.

Our friends were at their front door at that point, so we didn't discuss it further but went in. About halfway through the dinner, Ted looked over at me in utter amazement and whispered that it had just occurred to him that his back hadn't hurt him since we walked in the door!

George

GEORGE, fifty-eight years old, had several blockages in the arteries around his heart. He was taking several nitroglycerin tablets each day to stay alive. According to his doctor he was given three to six months to live, and when he called me, he was on his last month. He said he had nothing to lose and wanted to give spiritual healing a try.

The first week, I saw George three times. He was able to cut down on his nitroglycerin by a considerable amount. There were some days when he didn't need any. His color was improving and his breathing was better. For the next three weeks I saw him twice a week.

When I first started seeing George, he was a pretty gruff, unfriendly guy — sarcastic and critical of others. He seemed to have a "holier-than-thou" attitude. I saw psychically that he had a tremendous amount of fear. This fear was not of death; it was a fear of getting close to other people. He treated others gruffly so they wouldn't get too close. He was like a big, spoiled child. During our healing sessions, whenever my inner voice prompted me, I would talk to him about various issues he needed to work on. I was not acting as his therapist, telling him what I thought he should do — but passing psychic information on to him. Over the weeks, I talked to him about his sarcasm and his fears. We talked about his relationships with family members and the importance of healing those relationships.

George slowly began changing his attitudes. He became more considerate of others, more loving, more sensitive. A total change was taking place, and it was wonderful to witness. Each time we did a healing, he would open up a little bit more. I saw him for a total of three months. He lived a fairly active life (without nitroglycerin) for one more year.

Kathryn

KATHRYN TAUGHT ME quite a bit. She was twenty-six years old and had cancer in her right breast. The lump was underneath her arm. The first time I met her, I placed my hand under her armpit. The tumor was as big as my palm. She was sure she was going to be healed and back to perfect health.

I met with her once a week for about three months. She always showed improvement. The tumor was smaller each time I saw her. We became very close. We were about the same age and had similar life experiences.

One day after a healing session, we talked about what her life was going to be like when she was completely healed. We talked about her old job and her relationships with her boyfriend and her family. We talked about all the things she hadn't been able to do for so long and about her anxiety and fears of "returning to the normal world."

At about the end of the third month, I went on vacation for two weeks, and when I got back, I got a call from a mutual friend of ours who said that Kathryn had become very ill and wanted to see me as soon as possible. I jumped in the car and went to her home. She was lying on the couch, moaning in pain. She had lumps all over her neck. I had to pick her up and roll her over because she was too weak to do it herself. I was overwhelmed. I felt so helpless. I couldn't stand seeing her in such pain. I prayed hard for answers and felt guilty because I had left her for two weeks.

I went to her home the next couple of days and did more healings, but lumps were popping up everywhere. My inner voice kept saying something about a "fast," but I didn't understand what that meant. About the third day I asked her if she had fasted while I was in San Francisco. She said she had decided to clean out her system and had gone on an apple and water fast for those two weeks! She had lost thirteen pounds.

I was so angry and I was hurt. For weeks I had felt a real sense of comradeship with her in her healing process. Now I felt that was gone. She was no longer there with me. Why had she done this to herself? The fast seemed like she was starving herself — and such a contradiction to the healthy body we were striving for.

Don't misunderstand me. I'm not saying there's anything wrong with fasting. What I am saying is that the fast "felt" very inappropriate in this case. We were really making what appeared to be progress, and it seemed to me that in order to continue with the "flow" we were in, she needed to give her body proper nourishment. I realized at that point that I had become far too emotionally involved and that I had to separate our friendship from what was happening. Another part to all of this was that her family was becoming quite upset with me. They felt I was killing her. They didn't want me around her any more. She went to the hospital and died two weeks later.

A mutual friend called me to tell me to stay away from the funeral. The family was acting like they were on a "witch hunt" and were just waiting for me to show up.

I didn't go to the funeral. I was dealing with my own grief and confusion. I was angry with God. I was angry with Kathryn. I was angry that I even had this gift, and I told God that I was through. I would never do another healing as long as I lived. He needed someone tougher than I was — that was clear to me.

Two days later, I got a call from a friend of mine. Her stepson had fallen eighteen feet and landed on his head. He had been in a coma for weeks down in Nebraska, and they were flying him up to one of our major hospital centers. She asked if I would please do healings on him when he arrived in Minnesota.

Before I continue with this example and discuss how I returned to using the gift of channeling healings, I would like to share with you the important lessons I learned from working with Kathryn.

- It is important to stay detached from our clients. We can love them and care about them, but when we become personally involved, we lose a certain amount of good judgment that I believe is necessary to be a clear, non-interfering channel for healing.

- It is important to always remember we are not responsible for the outcome of anyone's healing process. We are the channel for it, not the power itself.

- Though we may think we know what is right for another person, in reality we cannot judge what other people need, or what is right for them. Again, we are a channel for healing energy, and that's it!

- It is important to remember that going from a restricted lifestyle due to bad health to a nonrestricted lifestyle with good health can be devastating to some people. Going from a long illness to good health is a major change and definitely a process.

- It is important to be grateful for each healing rather than always looking for the "end results." We learn our lessons on the journey. It's not about the destination.

- And remember, last but not least, death is always one of the healing options.

And now, back to Gary's story...

Gary

GARY, AGE FOURTEEN. As I said earlier, Gary had been in a coma for about two weeks when they flew him up from Nebraska to one of our major medical centers. I was still grieving Kathryn's death and did not want to do any more healings. Actually, I was afraid. I knew Gary's family fairly well. I guess you could say I had become gun shy. I was full of doubt and confusion. What if he died like Kathryn did? What if the family then held me responsible? I went in circles for a day, praying and yet not wanting to hear what my inner voice said.

Gary's family called several times to ask if I was willing to work with him. Then one morning when I was in the shower and my mind wasn't on any one thing in particular, out of nowhere I got a very clear vision of Gary lying in the hospital. I saw me sitting next to him with my hands on him, and my inner voice then said, "go!" With that came a real desire to do just that. So, within a couple of hours I was at the hospital. I have to admit to you that this was about eighteen years ago, and I don't remember all the details of Gary's recovery. But there are some I remember clearly that I think will be helpful to you when you are working with someone in a coma.

First off, when I arrived, a male nurse was telling the family that he doubted that Gary would ever come out of the coma, and that if by chance he did, he would very likely be unable to speak, walk, or ever take care of himself. He suggested that the family put him in a nursing home. That old doubt started creeping up in me. Right there I had to decide if I was going to hang on to the bleak diagnosis of the medical establishment or set myself apart from it and just do my job. I decided to leave the negativity outside of Gary's room and to trust in the healing energy.

I couldn't communicate with Gary so I ran my hands down his body about two inches above it, feeling for cold spots in his aura. Cold spots indicate where there's a problem with the body. There were cold spots everywhere. I prayed for direction. My inner voice directed me all the time.

About the third day of healings, I experienced something new. Gary's soul stepped out of his body and communicated with me. It was great! His soul knew every need that his body had. About the fifth day, his body started to respond. There was movement in his arms and legs.

He was moaning a little bit. The sixth day the doctors said they needed to operate on him. They said they needed to put a kind of bypass on his brain because the spinal fluids were not draining properly and the fluid was building up in his head. They said that without this device he would die. But his soul told me that his body was not strong enough for surgery, so I was to concentrate on putting a lot of energy everywhere to get him stronger. They wanted to do surgery that afternoon, and I was really worried that he wouldn't be strong enough. My inner voice, however, told me to calm down, that everything would be fine.

That afternoon, about an hour before they were going to take him to surgery, a strange substance showed up in his blood. My first thought was, "What the heck is going on?" My inner voice told me again that everything was going to be fine and to just concentrate on getting his body stronger.

They called all his relatives to the hospital to test their blood for this strange substance. They couldn't operate until they could identify it. No one knew what it was. They postponed surgery.

I did about three more healings in the meantime. The next day my inner voice told me that he was strong enough to go through surgery. That morning the strange substance mysteriously disappeared.

The operation was successful. The spinal fluids were flowing through the bypass. I continued to go to the hospital each day for about a week. Gary had come out of the coma. His speech was fine. He walked with a walker. He had a lot of adjustments to make: His pituitary gland had been permanently damaged, so he would need to take medication every day for that. He developed diabetes while in the coma. His vision was gone in one of his eyes. When I was working with his eyes, I saw a picture of blackness behind the eyeball, only blackness.

It felt as if there was nothing there at all. The family told me that when Gary was in Nebraska, the doctors had severed the nerves going to that eye because of a buildup of pressure. No wonder I was getting blackness! There was nothing there to work with.

Gary stayed in the hospital for about another month, mainly for rehabilitation. His legs needed to get stronger, and he had trouble swallowing food. After he was out of the coma, I went to the hospital another three times. Then it felt as if the healing was finished. I saw him about six months later. He was doing fairly well, living at home and back in school. The strange thing was that neither one of us knew the other six months later. He had gained weight, and his hair had all grown back. Until his mother introduced me, I didn't know that the young man walking around the kitchen talking baseball was Gary!

Dan

DAN WAS NINETEEN years old. He dove into a swimming hole, which turned out to be about three feet deep. He smashed his spinal cord and was paralyzed from the neck down.

Dan had been vacationing with family and friends on the West Coast when the accident happened. He had been in the hospital for about three days before I got the first call from his family. I started praying for absentee healing three times a day.

We were about two thousand miles apart, but I felt a strong connection with Dan. I had a strong feeling that I should go out and work on him directly but didn't have that kind of money. I prayed for an answer. The next day his family called to say that they wanted to pay my way out there if I was willing to come, so I canceled all appointments and took off for Oregon for a week.

I went to the hospital twice a day for the first three days. I placed my hands on his solar plexus when he was lying on his back. When they turned him over, we worked on his neck and spine. About the fourth day, he got a very bad bladder infection and a high fever, so for the next couple of days we worked on his bladder and worked a little on his arms and legs to get the energy flowing. About the fifth day, the bladder infection cleared up. He was beginning to raise his arms by himself. I continued to work on his neck, spine, and solar plexus. The seventh day found him feeling much better. He wiggled his right foot for me and was waving his arms around. His appetite returned, and he was doing much better mentally.

The week went by quickly, and it was time for me to get back to work in Minneapolis. I never saw Dan again, but I have gotten reports from his family that he left the hospital much earlier than was expected. He did not regain the use of his legs, and he uses a wheelchair, but he is in college, has his own apartment, and according to his family, is doing great.

Sharon

SHARON, AGE THIRTY-TWO, has genital herpes. Sharon's healing process was a little more involved than just physical healing. The first time she came for a healing, I placed my hands on her solar plexus and asked the energy to go wherever the body needed healing. I was told by my inner voice that Sharon needed to forgive the person who had given her the herpes and forgive herself for contracting the disease. Sharon had a lot of shame and guilt locked up inside. I was told she needed to release these negative feelings about herself.

Sharon came back a week later for another healing. My inner voice said she still needed to release more negative feelings toward herself and the person she contracted the herpes from, so I suggested she pray every day for forgiveness and again for the release of her negative feelings. I did another healing on her solar plexus, praying for the energy to completely heal the herpes.

Next, my guides suggested Sharon stop referring to the herpes as "my" herpes, but rather refer to it as "the" herpes. The last suggestion

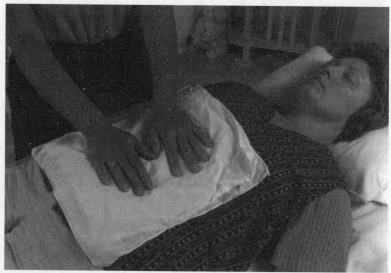

If it does not feel right to touch specific areas, I put both hands on the solar plexus area and again ask the energy to go where it needs to.

I gave Sharon was something I had learned at my church called "Affirm and Deny." I suggested that she deny the herpes if it recurred. Most people with herpes feel the onset of a breakout by sensations of burning, itching, and tingling. I told her that if she felt anything like these onset sensations to affirm, "I deny this herpes," thereby taking the power away from the disease.

Sharon called several months later to say she had not had any herpes since our last session.

Denying the Disease

I AM NOT SAYING that this kind of denial works in every case, but it can work. God can heal anything, if it's meant to be healed. But the suggestions given to Sharon were powerful: forgiveness, not owning the disease by referring to it as "mine," and taking the power of the illness away by denying it. Don't misunderstand me! I'm not saying to deny it in the sense of hiding your head in the sand and pretending it's not there. I mean, don't affirm the condition or its power...affirm instead your rejection of the condition's existence.

Think of it this way: Let's say someone you don't particularly care for shows up at your front door with luggage. This person informs you that they intend to visit you for ten days. Would you say, "Sure, come on in, I'll rearrange my whole schedule for you?" Or, would you put your foot down and say, "Sorry, I just can't accommodate you at this time." Hopefully you would be firm and not allow yourself to have this intrusion forced on you. Does it sound silly to compare something like this to herpes? An intrusion is an intrusion! Just put your foot down and tell those little cold sores they aren't welcome. Deny them. Don't affirm them.

Judy

JUDY, AGE THIRTY, said she felt a coldness in her abdomen. When she first came for a healing, she said she felt disconnected from herself. She was also low on energy. In general she was feeling all out-of-sorts but couldn't put her finger on anything specific.

I have done several healings on clients who come for an energy boost. I lay my hands on the solar plexus, do a twenty-minute healing, and pray to fill up the entire body with white light. Afterward, I put a spiritual shield on the solar plexus, which is discussed in the first chapter.

A number of my clients are therapists. Often, because of the nature of their work and because they open themselves up so much to their client's troubles, they end up feeling scattered or "burned out." Several have commented on how much clearer they feel after coming for a spiritual shield healing. They don't feel as vulnerable and don't exhaust their energy as they did before.

So when Judy told me what her needs were, I just figured it would be a one-time energy boost healing, ending with a psychic bandage. One of these days I'll learn! Once the healing began to flow, I could see Judy's uterus, very shriveled up and cold. It felt very cold. Judy cried through most of the healing. Psychically, it felt as though we had only just begun a process that was going to take quite some time.

Judy started coming every week for healings. Several different things were happening. She got in touch with her anger about being a woman. She realized she still had a lot of stored fear and resentment about being an incest victim. Each time she came for a healing, there was a lot of crying and releasing of these stored feelings.

There were many feelings surfacing that she didn't understand. My inner voice said it wasn't necessary for Judy to know what each feeling was, and that trying to understand every feeling was actually holding on to the feeling instead of letting it go. She should simply pray to release it.

In spite of all the tears and the inner emotional pain Judy was experiencing with her healing process, she was at the same time feeling much more connected with herself. She began to love herself in a very different way. The whole process took about eight weeks. It was a wonderful feeling the day she hugged me and told me she finally felt free. I felt truly grateful to have been able to participate in her healing process.

Janet

JANET, AGE TWENTY-EIGHT, had a urinary tract dysfunction for years. About three times a year she would go to her doctor to have her urethra stretched. She was pretty discouraged by the time she came to me for healings. She didn't have much confidence in laying-on-hands healings but said she was willing to try anything. During her sessions I would put both hands on her abdomen, praying that the healing energy would flow through to her urethra, making it whole and healthy again and dissolving the scar tissue that was causing the blockage.

Each time she had a healing, she would feel the relief for a couple of days, but then the pain would come back.

After about four weeks of doing healings on her "now and then," she called to say she wanted to start coming regularly until the problem was cleared up. I told her I would send absentee healings until we met again. That night as I was praying for absentee healing, my inner voice said that Janet did not feel worthy of being healed. I was rather surprised, because I thought I knew this woman pretty well, and it didn't seem to fit her. But I did call Janet in the morning to ask her about it. She immediately started to cry when I mentioned the word "worthy." She said that she did not feel worthy and that throughout the healings she had been afraid because she felt God was angry with her. She felt that some things she had done in the past had caused God to be angry with her and that her physical problem was her punishment. She actually feared God would make her problem worse!

We talked for quite a while on the phone that morning. The words that came to me during this conversation were: "Ask her to pray to feel worthy of healing."

I told her I would pray for her fear to be removed and asked her to pray that she would feel worthy of being a healthy person. We decided that when she was feeling worthy, she would get back to me. Three days later she called to say that she was ready, that she had done a lot of praying in those three days and that something inside her had changed.

I met with her that afternoon. The healing was quite unusual, and I think you'll find it very interesting. I placed my right hand on her abdomen. The heat came immediately. After about five minutes it literally felt like my hand had gone inside her stomach. It was the strangest sensation. I tried pulling my hand off her, but it was stuck as if it had been glued to her. Janet opened her eyes and yelled, "Your hand is inside me!" I told her that I could feel the same thing but that it was not inside. It was just stuck on her abdomen.

My inner voice was reassuring. It told me everything was fine and to just do my part. Janet and I could both feel "rearranging" going on inside. It was an amazing thing to feel. After about seven minutes we could both feel my hand slip out of her body, the energy stop flowing, and my hand become free to move. We both sat there in shock. We didn't know what to make of it. We sat and talked for quite a long while, and when I felt she was okay, I left. We have seen each other several times over the last few years, and she always tells me she's "still fine." After that healing day, she has never had another problem with her urethra. That was the only experience I ever had with that kind of healing.

Bob

BOB WAS IN HIS FIFTIES. He had lost his job and came for one healing because of depression. After the session he said he didn't want to spend any more money on this, so would I please send absentee healings. I said I would. I prayed for three days for healing on his depression. The fourth day Bob called. He wanted to know if I was still sending the healing. I told him that I was. He asked me to please stop. He said, "Things are starting to happen to force me to face my depression." He said he was kind of surprised, because he really hadn't expected it to work. But, since it was working, would I please stop since he didn't think he was ready to deal with all of it.

I felt badly for Bob because he seemed stuck in such a heavy place emotionally, but I stopped praying for absentee healing to him.

❖

Remember, when we pray for healing, a healing is going to occur on some level whether it's mental, emotional, physical, spiritual, or on a soul level. It's that old adage, "Watch out what you pray for. You might just get it!"

❖

Grace

GRACE WAS FULL OF ARTHRITIS. It was crippling her entire body. She came weekly for healings for about three weeks. Her fingers were straightening out a bit. She was able to walk a little without her cane.

Her energy was returning. One day she started to cry during the session. My inner voice said her body was actually crying because of what the arthritis had done to her. It was truly an emotional session for her. When she left she said she'd call, but I had a strong feeling that she wasn't coming back.

I could feel Grace was very embarrassed about crying in front of me. It felt like she was very afraid of her sadness. My sense was that she did not want to go any further with the healing process because she did not want to look at her body and its pain that closely. Some people would rather stay in denial of anything that is going on emotionally with them. I have had clients tell me they would rather die than look at the possible emotional roots of their physical problems.

Grace did not come back.

Ben

BEN HAD A HEART ATTACK about a year before I met him and was starting to have chest pains again. He was very frightened of having another attack. Ben was a very sweet and gentle man, and very respectful of healing.

The night I met with Ben and his wife, we first started to talk about healing energy and about our spiritual beliefs. I felt a certain apprehension from his wife but decided not to let it bother me. I prayed for a bubble of protection because I did not want to feel any of her negativity.

I placed both of my hands on Ben's chest. The healing energy was very intense. Ben cried quietly during the healing. He said he knew that God was healing him. He was so thankful afterwards and said he would call if he needed more. The next day I got a very brief phone call from Ben telling me that his wife was very concerned because I am not a "Charismatic," and he was sorry, but he couldn't come for any more healings. His wife's Charismatic Priest told her if I wasn't a Charismatic (a religious group), I wasn't a true healer because only Charismatics had the power to heal. I have heard this from other religions as well.

I was pretty upset, but knew there was nothing I could do. I had to let it go.

Henry

HENRY WAS EIGHTY-THREE years old when I met him. He wanted healing for chest pains and a low energy level. Every week for about five weeks Henry's wife, Mary, would drive him sixty miles to get his "treatment." He was a quiet man and very respectful of healing. He never had much to say except to let me know he was feeling better.

After our fifth visit together, Henry told me he felt he was healed. He said he was feeling like a young man of sixty. His chest pains were gone, and his energy level was back up to where he wanted it to be. He told me he'd call if he had a need for any more healing. Every year I receive a Christmas card from Henry and Mary, always with a note that Henry is doing just fine.

Jerry

JERRY WAS SIXTEEN years old when I met him. He was born with cerebral palsy. I remember clearly the fear I felt inside of me the night he walked up to me on crutches and asked me if I could heal his legs. He said he wanted to ride a horse, drive a car, and be like everybody else. I explained to him that the healing energy came from God, and that I needed to pray about it.

The fear I felt was that his condition might be karmic, and if it was, perhaps he was not ready to be physically healed. I believe God's will for Jerry was for him to walk free of the crutches and to live a "normal" life; but again, I believe Jerry's soul chose the cerebral palsy, and because of that I didn't know what to do. I assumed that because he was asking for the healing, perhaps he was done with the karmic lesson. But, as you know by now, my assumptions have not always been right, so I took it to God. I asked for a clear sign. Was Jerry ready to receive healing or not? The next morning I awoke with a vision of my hands on Jerry's legs, so I called him and we set up our first appointment.

Our first session was fairly uncomfortable. Jerry's mother was quite negative. She was sure her son would not be healed. In spite of her constant negative remarks, I continued to channel healings on Jerry's legs for about four weeks.

During this time I became aware of an American Indian spirit named White Horse working with me. I would channel energy into Jerry's head, and White Horse would stand at his feet pulling the energy down. There were so many breaks in the flow of Jerry's energy. Each week Jerry would give me a progress report. He felt his legs were getting stronger. He felt a lot of tingling in his legs. He was always very enthusiastic.

It's always nice when two healers work on someone at the same time. I suggest one hold the feet to ground the person so they will let more energy in. You need to listen to your intuition to guide you as to when to stop because two people channeling energy can be very powerful. I would not recommend this for everyone. If you have a feeling *not* to have two people work at the same time, *trust that.*

About the fifth week a friend of mine who also channels healing asked if he could work on Jerry with me. Together we worked on Jerry's legs, feet, and the flow of energy in his body and his upper torso. Several weeks passed from the first day I laid my hands on Jerry's legs. Slowly, we saw progress. We were all very excited. The night Jerry stood and took a few steps without his crutches, we all cheered.

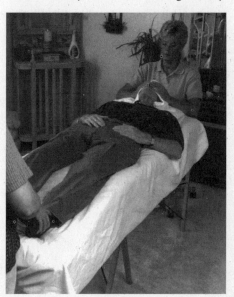

In all the weeks we worked together and talked about Jerry's expectations of his future without crutches, it had never occurred to me that this drastic change in his life style could be threatening to him mentally and emotionally. We talked to Jerry for quite a while about what life without crutches

Two healers working together

might be like. People would no longer think of him as "crippled." The expectations he might have, and that others might have of him, would change. We were so close, and yet something inside suddenly didn't feel right. My inner voice told me to back off and to give Jerry time to really think about his old way of life versus a new way of life. We told Jerry to think everything over very clearly and to let us know if he wanted to continue with healings. He never called me back.

Melody

MY DEAR FRIEND MELODY asked me if I would be in the delivery room with her when she gave birth to her second child. Her husband was too nervous to even think about being in there with her, and since I was with her when her first child was born, I really looked forward to the experience.

The baby was taking his time coming down the birth canal. Melody's face literally turned purple every time she tried pushing him down. I was standing by her side feeling totally helpless. It suddenly occurred to me to stand behind her, place my hands on her shoulders, and ask God to send energy into her body. I whispered to her that I was going to channel some energy into her and — pow! We both felt a bolt of energy go into her shoulders. She was able to relax, and right before our eyes, out came Shane. We looked at each other in sheer delight. She told me it literally felt like God lovingly pushed Shane out!

Kay

KAY RECENTLY CAME to me wanting her eyes healed. She has been near-sighted for years. She had been saying affirmations and praying that her eyes be healed, but she didn't feel like she was getting anywhere. She was concerned that her poor eyesight was an indication that there was something about herself she wasn't willing to see.

I placed one hand on her eyes and the other on her solar plexus. After channeling energy for about ten minutes, my inner voice told me to put one hand on Kay's throat area. I was told that the real root of Kay's bad eyesight was that she had seen many unpleasant things in her lifetime. I don't think this is unusual. But the problem started when

Kay wouldn't allow herself to voice her true feelings about the unpleasantness.

Kay had always been somewhat shy, and because of this she had always stifled her true opinions. My spirit guides said her feelings and opinions get stuck in her throat, causing throat problems. After the healing, I asked Kay if she had had throat problems, and she said that she had been bothered with them throughout her life.

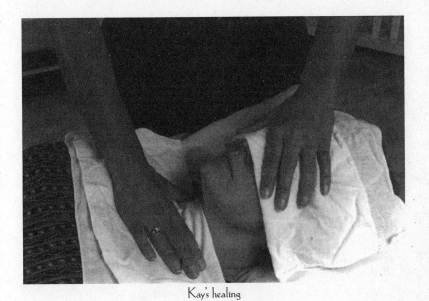

Kay's healing

Kay's eyes and throat were being affected because of her inability to voice her opinions.

Kay decided to discontinue healings for a time and to seek out an assertiveness class. We both feel that getting over the fear of talking about herself, her feelings, opinions, beliefs, et cetera, is very important to her health. She is continuing to say her affirmations every day, which are:

❖

I like what I see.
I clearly see the truth.
It is safe for me to tell the truth.
I express my feelings easily.

❖

Many times clients will ask me what they can do for their healing processes. Affirmations are very helpful. I really believe our attitude and visualizations play a very important role in our healing process.

Affirmations are simple, positive, and directed statements about ourselves, such as:

❖

I am a truly amazing person.
I am very capable.
I am learning to let myself grow.
I am very talented.
I am a very special person.
I am peaceful and calm.
I am learning to express my whole self.
I deserve to love and be loved.
I am a channel for healing.

❖

Say these affirmations to yourself three times a day for one month and notice how much differently you feel toward yourself and others.

I also suggest getting a copy of my second book, *Passion to Heal,* and doing the exercises at the end of each chapter. We need to free ourselves on all levels, and we can't really set the body free until we clear up our emotional issues, past and present.

Todd

TODD WAS A RUNNER. He was coming once a week for healings on his knees. His vacation was coming up, and he wanted his knees to be in tip-top shape for running along the beach. He called me one afternoon from California to say his knees were acting up, so I told him I would channel healing to him sometime that evening. The only time we could agree on was ten o'clock Minneapolis time (eight o'clock California time). Todd knew he'd be in a restaurant in San Diego at eight, having dinner with friends. At ten o'clock I sat down and visualized Todd sitting in a restaurant. I visualized my hands on both knees. I prayed for the healing and felt a connection. I thanked God for healing Todd's knees and went on about my business. Later that night Todd called. He apologized for calling so late, but said he just had to tell me what had happened. He said he was sitting and talking with his friends at the restaurant when all of a sudden he felt hands on his knees. He said his immediate reaction was to look at everyone's hands on the table, to see who was "playing around." He said he sat there kind of dazed because he couldn't figure out what was happening. Then it occurred to him that the healing was taking place. He looked at his watch, saw that it was 8:02, and started to laugh. He explained what was going on to his friends and said they were all curious and wanted to feel his knees. They could all feel the heat! Isn't that a fun story?

Jack

I SHARE THIS NEXT STORY with you in the hope that you'll read it and learn from it. I was pretty new to healing when I started channeling energy to Jack. I hadn't learned about detachment yet, or about my own boundaries. I still had the impression that all healings were supposed to heal a person totally. It hadn't occurred to me that the healing energy might simply be used to help a person be comfortable while they were in their death process.

One of my closest friend's father, Jack, had heart surgery, and during the surgery he had suffered a stroke. On my way to the hospital, I was praying for a sign as to what to do. I didn't get much of a feeling about anything. I didn't get yes, I didn't get no. His family desperately wanted him to be healed. I became emotionally involved right away. I saw the fear on their faces. "I" wanted to fix the situation. For the most part, I dropped everything in my own life and went to the hospital every day. A couple of times when he would go back on the critical list I would stay overnight at the hospital. I didn't separate myself at all and stayed emotionally hooked in with everyone else. Some days we would see progress, only to have something new go wrong the following day.

One Sunday afternoon, while I sat next to Jack's bed channeling a healing, my solar plexus suddenly started jerking. It felt like something was ripping my insides out. I couldn't get it to stop. I prayed for an understanding of what was happening. I heard someone walk up behind me. It was the spirit I mentioned earlier: White Horse. He told me to get out of the room and get out of the hospital. He was very firm. He repeated it over and over. After seeing White Horse during many of the healings I had channeled, I had come to trust what he had to say.

So I got up and left the room. I couldn't walk standing straight. I was hunched over in pain, my solar plexus continuing to jerk. I went down to the family room and told my friend I had to get out of the hospital. She called a psychic in town and asked him if he knew what the jerking was. The psychic said I was channeling my own life's energy to Jack and that I had become so involved with him that I was giving up my own energy to keep him alive.

If you skimmed over that last paragraph, please go back and read it again. It was a frightening experience, and one I hope you won't have to go through. I left the hospital, went home, and went to bed. That afternoon the family called to say Jack had had a heart attack. They asked me if I would please come up to the hospital. My inner voice said no — very loudly. The next day I went to a healer friend of mine to get a healing on myself. He helped me to see what I was doing. He told me I had to detach myself, that I was not responsible for Jack's wellness, that I couldn't allow myself to be affected by what everyone wanted for Jack. He told me that maybe Jack's soul was trying to leave his body. Those were important words for me to hear.

I continued to channel energy to Jack for about four more days. I was not channeling the energy with that desperate feeling of "Live!" I was channeling the energy to relieve the physical pain he was in. On a Thursday afternoon I went to the hospital to do a healing on him. I placed my hands on his chest and nothing came out of my hands. My inner voice told me Jack had made his decision and that he would be leaving his body, soon. He passed away that night.

Chapter 12

The Most
Miraculous Healing

When I give talks on healing, I am often asked to describe the most miraculous healing I have ever seen.

Without a doubt, the most miraculous healing I have ever been involved in happened with my own sister, Nikki.

It was one of the best experiences I have gone through as a healer. I learned many valuable lessons that I would like to share with you.

Nikki was twenty-nine years old at the time she got sick. She was the healthiest member of our family. She never smoked, she exercised regularly, and I can't ever remember a day she called in sick at work. Her attitude was always that she didn't have time to be sick, so when she first started complaining that she couldn't breathe very well, none of us thought it was very serious. Even the doctors in the emergency room minimized her breathing problem. They sent Nikki home with antibiotics, not sure what was wrong. The next day she was taken to the hospital in an ambulance. She was first diagnosed with double pneumonia and admitted into the hospital.

After ten days on antibiotics, Nikki suddenly got worse. X-rays indicated both lungs were collapsing. She was rushed into surgery to inflate the lungs and also to do a biopsy on the lung tissue.

The results were devastating. She had a rare lung disease called Hammond-Rich Syndrome. There was no known cause or cure. The doctor told us the next two weeks were critical and told us to try to stay as positive as possible although the disease was considered fatal.

It seemed as if overnight my healthy twenty-nine-year-old sister went from jogging every day to lying completely still in intensive care, dependent on several medications, including steroids and an oxygen

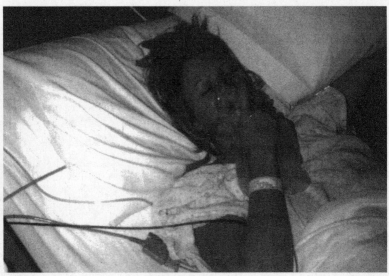

Nikki in intensive care

mask, twenty-four hours a day to keep her alive. The doctor told us she would probably never leave intensive care but if by chance there was some kind of miracle and she did leave the hospital, she would probably go to a nursing home where she could be taken care of. He said she would never be able to walk the length of a room or sit up in a chair for very long. I remember the day she asked me to wash her hair while she lay in bed. She had to move her body up to the head of the bed so we could use a special tray, and this exertion completely exhausted her for the rest of that day and the next. It was so hard to accept that she was as sick as she was, but there was proof all around us that she was really struggling.

Up until her surgery, Nikki and I had never discussed my healing gift. Maybe this was because she had always been healthy and there was no need to discuss it. Maybe it was because she wasn't on her spiritual path yet and didn't feel comfortable talking about it, but for whatever reason, we never talked about it.

When she came out of surgery, she wrote me a note that said, "Heal me." I started channeling healings to her that day. That's when my next level of learning lessons around being a healer began. They were some of the toughest lessons I've had to learn. I did not want to go through them, but I am grateful today for the experiences.

The biggest lesson I was continually reminded of was that as a channel for healing, I have no control of the healing, the person's healing process, or its outcome.

Every day I went to the hospital to channel healing to Nikki, but my hands would only heat up for one hour every other day. Even though I spent at least eight hours a day at the hospital and even though during those eight hour days I would ask God to please send healing through more often, my hands would only heat up every other day for one hour.

There was a period of three days when my sister went into a depression. She was quite despondent. She didn't want to talk or eat and just stared at the wall. The doctor told me he was really worried about her, and I remember him saying that if we were a family that believed in prayer, now was the time to pray.

During those three days, my hands would not channel any energy. I begged God but nothing happened. I made deals with Him. I cried. I got mad and yelled. Nothing could get my hands going. Nothing.

I called my minister. He was sleeping, but his wife and I had a wonderful conversation. She said it sounded like my sister's soul was possibly making a decision about whether it was time for her to go or not and that I needed to work on accepting whatever choice her soul made.

In this case, accepting the things I could not change might mean letting go of my baby sister. It was one of the worst nights of my life! I asked my then husband how someone lets go of someone they love very much. I sat up until four o'clock that morning, crying and wondering how to pray for my sister, and for myself. Do I pray for my sister's complete healing? Do I pray for God's will to be done? What was God's will? I was really mad at God for not taking all this pain away and for not sending healing through my hands. I wondered what good it was to have this gift if I couldn't even help my own sister live.

The next morning I woke up and felt a peacefulness inside. I went up to the hospital earlier than I usually did, and I remember when I got to the front door of the hospital, my hands heated up. When I got to my sister's room, she was lying in bed with a big smile on her face. She said, "Hey, you got any healing in those hands?" and I immediately started channeling an hour-long healing to her.

About a week later, they moved Nikki out of intensive care and into a regular ward. Each day she was improving. Externally she was looking and sounding better. Internally her tests were continually improving.

We celebrated her 30th birthday in the hospital. We had a lot to celebrate because the doctor told us that if she had someplace to go where someone could take care of her, she could leave the hospital!

She moved in with my husband and me, and I continued to channel healing every other day. Slowly, she got off all medications. Each day she would go for longer periods of time without the oxygen mask, until one day she no longer needed any oxygen or any medications.

She asked her doctor if she could go back to work and if she could start exercising. Her doctor advised against it. He felt the disease had probably gone into remission and didn't want to set up any stress on the body that could kick the disease off again. But Nikki felt strongly that she was ready to go back to her life.

She began slowly, going back to work part time. She started jogging again, a little at a time. Her body went into a depression from coming off all the drugs, and as she slowly came up out of the depression, she realized she wanted her life to be different. She had always wanted to be a flight attendant, and again against her doctor's orders, she applied and got the job. She was getting stronger and stronger each day.

It has been twelve years since that experience and my sister is doing very well. She just had a lung X-ray two weeks ago, and the doctor told her her lungs looked just fine. She's engaged to be married to a great guy and is still a flight attendant. She's on a spiritual path and takes it very seriously. It truly was the most miraculous healing I have ever been involved with.

I would like to get back to the lessons I learned from this experience. I've already discussed the realization that I have no control as a channel for healing. Even though my will for the person I am working on is that they physically, mentally, and emotionally heal from whatever problem they are having, I cannot get my will in there. I have to let go of their healing process and the outcome of that process. The journey and the final outcome of the healings is between the person's soul and God.

Nikki in September 1995

The other very valuable lesson is that even though I am grateful to be one of the channels that God worked through with my sister's healing, I would not recommend working on family members. It is very stressful. It's also very difficult to separate and detach from our emotions and our desires for our loved ones so that we can listen to our inner voice and let it guide us with the healing. This may sound contradictory because I have advised you to practice on family members and loved ones, but what I'm talking about here is that I think it's best, when there's a life-and-death situation like this one, that we bring in another healer who can be objective about listening to their intuition and hearing what the person needs.

That was probably the most difficult part of this whole experience as the channel for healing. I knew I had to detach myself totally so I could hear whatever guidance I was receiving. Doing so was very difficult.

If you have a loved one who is very ill, and you are the only channel around, then you will need the discipline to go inside to the center of yourself and ask God daily, maybe minute by minute, to help you stay focused on Him and His direction — rather than on what your loved one or other members of your family are saying. You have to be a clear channel if you're really going to help them.

If you are fortunate enough to have other healers in your area who you can call on, I would suggest that. They can be a lot more objective with your family than you can.

Through this experience with Nikki, I also learned compassion for the desperation of family members and loved ones. I have had many calls over the years from frantic family members begging me to drop everything and get to the hospital right away. Through this experience I saw and felt firsthand what that franticness was like. I called my healer friend, Alberto Aguas, and begged him to drop everything and please come to Minnesota to heal my sister. I wanted someone to come and fix my sister now. Praying suddenly didn't seem enough.

As my minister's wife said, at times like these we want a God with skin on. We want to reach out to someone in a body who is as close to God as possible and have them fix whatever is wrong. It's human to want that, but let me make a suggestion if you find yourself in a position where someone desperately needs healing and you can't get to them. Pray for absentee healing. Or tell their family members or loved ones to go and touch their sick friend and ask God to send the energy through them. We all have the ability to channel healing. It's simply a matter of asking the healing energy to come through us for our loved one's highest good. God gave all of us the gift of healing so we could reach out and touch those people in need of it.

I can hear some of you thinking, "Is she saying we are all healers?" What I'm saying is that we all have the gift to channel healing to someone who is suffering. No, I don't believe we are all meant to be spiritual healers, but we all can channel spiritual healing.

Chapter 13

Other Sources of Healing

When I mail a new client letter out to clients coming in for the first time, I also include a list of health-care practitioners here in Minneapolis who I have personally worked with. This gives people additional options in their healing process. It was very important for me to realize that I am not the only source available to help people heal.

I think that because of the work Jesus did, we have the idea that spiritual healing should be instantaneous and the only thing necessary. If that were true, we'd just have spiritual healers and wouldn't need doctors, nurses, masseuses, therapists, astrologers, prayer and meditation, the clergy, acupuncturists, osteopaths, chiropractors, kinesiologists, reflexologists, iridologists, psychics, nutritionists, shamans, rolfers, biofeedback, and so on. The list of potentially helpful health-care practitioners is long — it goes on and on.

If you believe that people don't need anything else but you, you're cheating people out of possibly getting valuable help from other channels of healing. Also, you don't need that burden of responsibility on your shoulders.

Please, if you do have this belief, let it go. You are not the only one that can help people.

We are mind, body, and spirit. We have bodies, emotions, and soul issues. There are usually many layers to heal in order for total healing to take place.

Hopefully, you've been in or are in your own healing process, so you should know people in your area who would be good for your clients to see. Many different things may come up during a healing session, i.e., incest memories, abuse issues, physical pain, past life memories, and pain. You may sense that the client has allergies or need to detox in order for their healing process to work. I would suggest you put together a list of other good, reputable health-care practitioners in your area so that you can give it to your clients if they ask for a referral to someone.

Remember, it is not healthy for us to think we are all people need. It can be limiting for their process and very hard on us to try to be all things for all people.

Chapter 14

God Is In Charge

Periodically throughout my childhood, and beginning as far back as I can remember, at age four or five, I heard a voice tell me to learn everything I could about Jesus.

I remember being seven and hearing this voice tell me one Sunday morning to get up and go to Sunday School because I needed to hear about Jesus.

I loved hearing about him. The stories. The parables. The Sermon on the Mount. His gift of healing. His faith in God. Then and now, I love hearing about this very brave and dedicated man.

I didn't know for a long time why it was so important for me to know about his life, his attitude, his miracles. To this day I am in awe of the task he took on and accomplished.

My former minister, Rev. Philip Laporte, said in a sermon that Jesus was not ordained by anyone in order to have his ministry. He answered a call from God.

Many times in my work and in my life when I come up against something that seems pretty hard to deal with, I go to that calm place within myself and ask how Jesus would have handled the situation. The answers that come are amazing.

Jesus has been a great role model for me. Personally, I see him as my older brother who came here to teach me and everyone else how to live our lives. If you're wondering if I'm a reborn Christian trying to sneak up on you from behind and convert you, that's the last thing on my mind, and no, I am not a reborn. I've been reborn many times throughout my life, but as far as following the reborn religion, no. I'm just sharing this with you so you will know who my spiritual teacher is and has been.

Being a spiritual healer is not about graduating from a ten-week course or several healing courses. It's not about how many certificates you can acquire.

If you have a desire in your heart to be a healer, God put that desire in your heart. You are a spiritual healer.

As you saw in this book, the healing techniques I use were covered in the first chapter. The rest of the book has been about dealing with illness, with people, and with the many facets of ethics. We've also looked at boundaries, dependency, ego problems, fees, and taking care of ourselves.

In and of itself, spiritual healing is very simple. It involves laying our hands on people and asking God to send healing energy through us. Then we must open up, get out of the way, and allow the energy to flow through our bodies, our arms, our hands. That's spiritual healing. It's simple, it's incredibly powerful, and it works!

Human pain and suffering are what can make spiritual healing complex. Dealing with the medical profession and science can bring in doubt and confusion. The need for illness causes skeptics to question the validity of spiritual healing.

Take an illness, give it a dose of spiritual healing, and it will heal. Add the human drama, and you need to buckle up your seat belt because the road suddenly becomes bumpy!

Let me give you an example of what I'm talking about.

Five months ago a very good friend of mine, thirty-nine years old, found out he had stomach cancer. The doctors went in to remove the tumor and said it was almost the size of a football and was so entangled with everything inside that they had to leave it there. They said this was a rapidly growing tumor so they were going to take a very aggressive approach and give him heavy doses of chemotherapy for a year. They said they would know in a year if he was going to make it or not.

My friend was in the hospital for about four weeks, and almost every day I channeled a very strong hour-long healing to him. There were some days when the healings were so strong that he would ask me to take my hands off because his whole body had become very hot.

A few times he made the comment at the end of the healing, "Thank God you're done, I don't think I could've taken much more." I must say there were times I wondered how much longer I could keep going because the energy coming through me was so intense.

Every day I felt strongly guided to go to the hospital to channel these healings. They felt so important.

The night before my friend left the hospital, I channeled a very strong healing for at least an hour, and when I finished, it felt like I was done channeling healings to him! My intellect thought I was crazy because it seemed like we had a long way to go (the doctors had said it would be a year of chemo, right?), but my inner voice said, "There, that's it." Hmm . . . I wasn't sure what that meant, but I left the hospital that night feeling such an inner peacefulness.

My friend went home from the hospital and for a couple of months has been dealing with chemo, hospitals, doctors, nurses, aches and pains, changes in his lifestyle, and all of the fear and anxiety that goes along with the uncertainty of cancer.

My inner voice continued to say no when I asked it about channeling him another healing.

About three weeks ago, my friend started having pains in his colon. An ultrasound was done and the doctors said the tumor was growing. We were all surprised; he had been doing so well.

My friend ended up back in surgery for an obstruction in his bowel, and I would say this was a blessing in disguise. Once the doctors were inside, they saw the tumor had in fact shrunk considerably. It appeared so much bigger in the ultrasound pictures because of scar tissue that had formed on the tumor, but the tumor itself was much smaller. That's not the best part. They took another biopsy of the tumor, and it was now benign!

This had been a rapidly growing tumor, and now it was rapidly shrinking. The doctors had said it would be a year before they knew if my friend was going to make it or not. Because they had not been able to remove this football-sized tumor, we all wondered if he would be alive in a year. Yet, five months later, he had a shrunken and benign tumor instead of a rapidly growing, cancerous one!

I asked my friend what the medical staff said about it. He said four doctors were trying to explain to him how this happened but said they couldn't other than that he must have really taken well to the chemotherapy. My friend said that one of his nurses said she didn't believe the new tests and that he still needed to realize he's living on borrowed time.

Can you see the point of my story? Take the healing energy. Give it to the physical problem. It's going to do what it does best: HEAL. It's perfect. Pure. Simple. Powerful. Then you add all the humans and each of their beliefs and personal dramas, and the actual miracle taking place gets lost.

If my friend hadn't had the second surgery that showed the tumor had shrunk, I wonder what he would have subconsciously done with the ultrasound results two weeks prior that said the tumor was growing. I suspect that in spite of the fact that he was actually improving, this information would have led his mind to do a real number on him. He would likely have been convinced that he was getting worse each day, and the medical staff would have treated him like someone who was declining instead of improving. Who knows where all that would have led?

I've seen this kind of thing over and over again. If the doctor says the patient is getting better, they continue to do so. If the doctor says the patient doesn't have much longer, has a worsening condition, or will be dead within days or weeks, oftentimes their prognosis comes true.

That's why we as channels for healing cannot get caught up in the fears and negative thinking of the world. We have to listen to our inner voices. Mine knew what was going on with my friend, and it never wavered. It knew the healing energy was going in and doing what it was meant to do: heal the problem.

Some of you might be wondering about people you know or have known who did not heal from spiritual healings. The healing energy did not fail them. Remember there are many reasons for illness and disease, and many times when death is also a healing.

We never know what form the healing will manifest.

People are forever trying to figure the healing energy out. We try to manipulate it, intellectualize it, and control it. But I have found over and over again that I am simply the channel. We are all simply channels. And no matter how much we try to complicate it with our theories or techniques, with our beliefs, and with our preconceived notions of what it's supposed to be, it works in spite of us.

I'd like to share another story with you to emphasize this point.

I had a client who came for a healing on her eyes. She didn't want to wear her glasses anymore. She didn't mention anything else, so I sat up at her head and channeled energy into her eyes for about forty minutes. She lay there for some time before she "came to."

As she was putting on her coat to leave, she turned to me and told me she was going to the hospital the next day to have several cysts removed from her uterus and asked if I thought the healing could have done anything to the cysts.

I told her that I am never 100 percent sure where the healing energy goes and that she might want to get another ultrasound before they do surgery.

She called the next day to say she did get another ultrasound and it showed there were no cysts so they canceled surgery.

Her body had its own agenda. I think it's safe to say that my client's body did not want surgery, so when the healing energy came in, the cysts and not the eyes were its number one priority because her eyes didn't improve at all!

This work is so humbling because it continually reminds me that even though I may think I know what's going on, realistically I don't.

There is an exchange of healing energy going on between God and the person receiving the energy. That's all we know for sure. And even

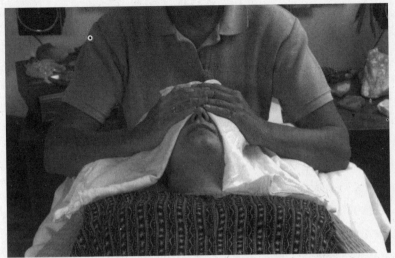

We may think we know where the energy is going or how the healing is working, but we really don't know any of it for sure. We are the channels; God is the healer.

that varies from healer to healer. Not all healers believe it comes from God. Most are in agreement that it comes from a divine source, but we all vary in our beliefs.

I would strongly suggest that if you are going to use your gift of healing that you go within to find your own beliefs about where it comes from — not only for your own knowingness but because many people will be asking you.

I would like to share something that a friend of mine, Rev. Paula Sunray Culp, put in one of her newsletters. I've got it hanging on the wall in front of my desk because it helps me stay focused on my work and my purpose.

What Is an Ordained Person?

SOMEONE WHO REMEMBERS who they are. Someone who is committed to spiritual principles in their life and prioritizes time so that they can develop their own spirituality. Being ordained does not necessarily mean standing behind a podium. It means that you are willing to step into your own Christhood and feel ordained in the eyes of God as well as feeling a deeper spiritual connection with the people in your life. Your approach to your relationships, family, and job can be a ministry in itself.

The other words that help me a lot as a healer are the words of Jesus found in Matthew.

Jesus knew that he personally did not carry the full weight of his work. The greatness of his father was ever available and unceasingly at work. Jesus knew that he alone could do nothing, but that he was, most surely, the channel, the appointed person. Through him, God's work would be done.

I wish the very best life has to offer you as you travel down your journey as a spiritual healer.

He let the greatness of God take over.

Conclusion

In the spring of 2003, the former publisher of this book, ACS Publications, reverted rights back to me because of changes they were making in the company. Fortunately, my main publisher, New World Library, decided to pick it up.

The acquisitions director, Georgia Hughes, went through the book with a fresh perspective. She moved a few things around and ordered a brand new cover, which I love. I asked Georgia if I could write a new ending because I wanted to give you an update on the style of healings I'm doing today and also include any information I've learned since the last update in 1997. I was certain that there was new information to share with you, but after rereading the book, I realized that this simple book covers everything you'll need to know in order to channel healing energy. I've already discussed the importance of using white hankies when channeling healing, covered the topic of absentee healings, and said that most often I've seen faster results with absentee healing than "in-person" healing. I've covered the subject of keeping our egos in check by always remembering where the energy comes from and discussed the importance of taking care of ourselves so as not to burn out. We've looked at ethics, boundaries, working with people, and the importance of finding a balance in our own lives. Throughout the book I make it pretty clear that it's very important to keep healing simple. You're going to be developing a stronger, deeper relationship with your Higher Power and also learning to trust your intuition, your hands, and the wisdom that works through them, but you'll still need to keep it simple.

In addition to all that, I've also shared with you details of my journey from the beginning when I first discovered that I had the gift of healing to my full-time practice as a spiritual healer. Perhaps the next logical place to go here is to offer an update on my career.

In 1997, I made a very difficult decision to stop seeing clients on a one-to-one basis. Thirty-two years ago the nerves in my arms were permanently damaged in a car accident. Over the years I've done a variety of things to help them heal, including physical therapy, cortisone injections, acupuncture, massages, chiropractic care, lymphatic drainage, and healings. Every one of them gave me temporary help, but after a while, the pain always came back.

This constant pain in my arms finally forced me out of a successful career as a barber, but this turned out to be a blessing because that opened the door to my new career as a psychic and spiritual healer. Then, in 1997, there I was, twenty years later, faced with the same decision about what to do with the pain in my arms. It was my acupuncturist that suggested I take some time off from doing healings and give my arms a chance to heal. She said that the fact that my arms weren't healing permanently was actually another blessing in disguise and that I should be open to new possibilities. I'll never forget the feeling I had when she said that. I felt as if God was speaking directly to me through her.

Even so, it was a very difficult decision for me to make. I had worked hard to establish a reputable name as a spiritual healer in a world that wasn't open to it. Letting it go didn't happen over night. I met with my minister a few times to help me get settled with the idea. I sought out my psychic friends and astrologer for their advice. I consulted my intuition endlessly, trying to get some clear guidance, and all any of them could tell me was that it was now time to shift gears and "heal the masses."

It's taken some time to understand what "healing the masses" meant, but slowly the pieces started falling into place, and I began to see how to use my healing gift.

How I Channel Spiritual Healing Today

BEFORE I DIVE IN to the four ways I now channel healing, I'd like to digress a bit and talk about touch. Many of you might find this hard to believe, but for most of my life I haven't been a real touchy-feely sort of person. Touching the people closest to me always made me feel vulnerable, and I didn't like it.

When I started channeling healings, touching people was awkward for me. As I got used to channeling healing, I found touch to be very comforting both to the client and myself.

Sometime in the late 1980s our consciousness was changing about touch. We started hearing a lot about "bad touch," and people became paranoid about touching one another. Unfortunately, we became a society afraid to touch each other.

I saw a change in the healers I knew. Some stopped touching their clients and would channel the energy three to six inches above the body so that their clients wouldn't misinterpret their touch as a sexual advance.

Then in the early 1990s, the pendulum started to swing back the other way. We were no longer just hearing about "bad touch," but the professionals began talking about "good touch" as well as the concept of boundaries or personal space. Slowly people began to calm down a bit about touching each other, and I think we're still struggling to figure out what's appropriate touch and what isn't.

When I was seeing clients one-on-one, I could always sense if someone was uncomfortable being touched, and I would ask them if they preferred that I not touch them during the healing. However, most clients were grateful to be touched in a nonsexual, healing way, and many remarked that during a healing was the only time they received any positive touch in their life and they loved it.

I've already stated earlier in the book that it's important not to cross personal boundaries and touch people when they haven't asked, so when the Universe started to work through me in a new way, it took some getting used too. I would be walking through a public place, and my right hand would literally move on its own to someone's back or shoulder. I would feel the healing energy shoot into their body. Most of the time it happened so fast I wouldn't be aware of it until the quick shot of healing was over. I might be standing in line at the airport or grocery store; it didn't matter where I was. Once I was standing in line at the video store, juggling my purse, videos, and other packages, and my right hand jetted out from my body and landed on the back of the person in front of me in line. The woman had been coughing badly and nonstop. As soon as my hand shot her some healing energy, she stopped coughing. She turned around with an inquisitive look on her face (probably to say why do you have your hand on my back), and I just smiled and said, "Excuse me."

Sometimes I've tried stopping my hand from going where it wants to go because I am so conscientious of not violating people's boundaries, but spirit always has a way of letting me know who's still in charge. Such was the case with an elderly woman I saw one day at the drugstore. She was slowly walking around with her walker, looking for a certain battery. She told the young girl behind the counter that she was eighty-four years old and it wasn't easy getting around. She asked if the clerk would help her. My right hand started filling up with healing energy, and I could feel it wanted to move to the woman's shoulder. I didn't want to scare her, so I kept it in my pocket. My inner voice chimed in and said to give the woman some healing energy, but I went into my head and started worrying about crossing her personal space.

The young girl told her they were all out of that particular size but to try the grocery store across the mall. I was struggling with what to do. Should I butt in and offer to drive her to the store, or since I was headed to the same grocery store, should I offer to pick up the batteries and bring them back here so she didn't have to schlep over there? My hand was full of healing energy, and my inner voice was still pushing, and I was still resisting.

I decided to finish shopping at the drugstore and pay for my items. By the time I was done, I thought, I would know what to do. It couldn't have been more than five minutes when I went outside, and she was nowhere in sight. As I was driving to the grocery store, I was reprimanding myself for not channeling the healing to her. I walked into the store, and who do you suppose was standing there with her walker? There is absolutely no way that woman could have gotten there that fast, but she did. I immediately went over to the battery section and got the size she was looking for. I walked over to her, put my right hand on her shoulder, and asked her if this was what she was looking for. She stared at my hand on her shoulder and got this huge smile on her face. She told me I was an angel and thanked me for the batteries. As I headed for the lettuce, I thanked God for not letting me get in the way any longer than I did.

It's not always sweet little old ladies or sick children that God ministers to. The next experience I want to tell you about had the potential to be quite ugly.

A friend and I were driving back to my house one night, and I had my high beams on. Up over the hill came a car, going very fast. I quickly tried switching my lights over to regular beam, but without realizing it, I switched back to the bright lights. He drove past my car, screaming obscenities at me about being an old lady and to get off the road. I looked in the rearview mirror, and I saw these reverse lights coming right at me at a very fast speed. I turned left onto my street and pulled into my driveway. He came to a screeching halt at the corner and was out of his mind with rage.

Normally, in a situation like this, my blood pressure would have been off the charts, and I would have sat in the car until he left, but I felt my hands heat up, and I felt intuitively led to get out of the car and talk to the young men.

I motioned to him to come here. My friend was telling me to get back in the car. My neighbor was hollering not to get involved, but I was listening to my inner voice. I felt completely surrounded in God's grace as I walked over to the two young men screaming at me from their car. My right hand immediately went to the young man sitting in the passenger seat. Their car reeked of alcohol. In a very calm voice I asked them what was wrong and why they were so upset. The driver said that I tried to blind them, and very calmly I explained that I got so nervous I accidentally turned the high beams on instead of off and that I was really, really sorry. The energy was pouring out of my hand, and I believe it wasn't going into the passenger only; I believe it was going into the car as well. The driver told me I needed to calm down, and I told him I wasn't the one who was upset and that he needed to calm down, but the tone of my voice was so soft and gentle that both of them seemed mesmerized by it. Within seconds, they were both telling me they were sorry and they didn't know what had come over them. Then, they told me to have a nice evening and drove away. I walked away feeling like I was wrapped in God's grace, and that feeling stayed with me for the rest of the night.

About half the time, my hand works on its own, not giving me a clue that it's about to touch someone. Other times, my inner voice gives me a heads up that we're about to channel healing to someone. It's always a gentle touch on the shoulder or back and never any place else. I say something short and sweet, such as, "Have a nice day," or compliment them in some way, and then I move on. As my minister Ken Williamson always says, "We're how God gets around." That's how I see these quickie healings. God is simply using one of his/her instruments for healing.

Another way that the energy has been working through me is when I give a lecture. Here's a great example of what I'm talking about. I was doing a book signing at Borders bookstore. During the question and answer portion of my talk, a woman in the audience asked if I would channel healing to everyone as I was giving my talk. I closed my eyes and asked the Universe to please send healing out to whoever was open to receive it, and then I went on with my talk. We figured there had to have been at least 150 people there that night, so I was curious how many people would experience healing. After the talk, several people came up to me who had been standing all over the store and told me that they came in with various physical ailments such as headaches, sore throats, aching hips, and sinus infections. Each of them told me that shortly after they started receiving the energy, they felt restored to health. One woman told me she was standing at the back by the door in case her headache got so bad she had to leave. Instead, the headache was completely gone.

The other way I've learned to channel the energy is that after I've given a lecture or taught a workshop, I end the day with a guided meditation. Facing the crowd, I open up my hands and ask God to please channel healing energy to everyone that's open to receive it. I make it part of the meditation, with beautiful music playing in the background. People love it. I always get great feedback after the lecture.

The other form of healing I continue to do is absentee healing, which is discussed in chapter 1, but I've learned a different way to do them. Here's a great story for you and a picture to go along with it. First a little background: In January of 2003, I opened a teaching and healing center in Bloomington, Minnesota. My friend Melody Beattie has a bookstore in the center. On October 6, 2003, I was teaching a beginners healing class. My assistant, Nancy, called Melody to see if she was coming over to the center because one of the students wanted to talk to her about a book. Mel told her that she had burned herself badly on her fireplace and that she wouldn't be going anywhere. She asked Nancy to have me send an absentee healing. As soon as Nancy gave me the message, I said a quick prayer for healing and went on with class. During break I called Mel to see how she was doing, and she said that even though it was just one finger that got burned, it felt like her entire hand was on fire, so I told her I would pray for more healing. When I got off the phone, I closed my office door and stood in the middle of the room. I said out loud, "God, you and I are one," and I immediately felt an energy surge throughout my body. Then I said, "Now let's become one with Melody and heal her." Another surge went through my body. It was very strong, and when I opened my eyes, I felt dizzy from it. I sat for about a minute until the fuzziness left my head, and then I went back to class. I had never channeled absentee healing like that before and wondered how I knew to do that.

After class, I called Melody to see how she was, and she said that ever since we talked, she felt stoned. She said she was "out of it" and was going to go to bed.

The next morning I called to see how she was doing, and she answered the phone in a great mood. She said she was fine and her finger was fine. There was no blistering. Just happy as a clam, I made a comment about God being so cool, and we moved on to other subjects.

Later that afternoon, her cleaning lady asked Melody what had happened to her brand new blanket. Seems there was a big hole blown out of it. At first Melody had no idea why her cream-colored quilt now had a big hole in it with a pinkish color surrounding the edge of the hole. There was also another tiny little hole about four inches away from the big hole. She called to tell me this story, and it dawned on both of us that this must have had to do with the healing the night before. When she showed me the blanket, it was obvious that the hole was an imprint of her hand. She told me she was holding this blanket to rest her finger on when I prayed for the healing. Here's a picture of

Melody's blanket

it so that you can see for yourself. The little hole at the top of the picture is where her thumb was.

Being a part of this magical gift of healing is the absolute coolest gift ever. I don't know what people need. I don't know where they're at in their healing process. I am and you are simply the channels that God uses to get this healing energy out to people. Our job ALWAYS is to listen to our inner voice for guidance, and we can't go wrong.

God Bless You,
Echo

Note to Readers

A note to those of you who may have purchased this book, not to learn to be a healer but because you are looking for healing for yourself or someone you love, I have an option for you at www.echobodine.com called Healing Pen Pals.

I teach a sixteen-week laying-on-hands healing class, and whoever wants to continue on in their healing studies joins the Advanced Healing Class. When I receive a request for healing, my assistant, Nancy, gives one of the Healing Pen Pals that person's name, location, and what they would like healing for. That student sends absentee healing to that person every day for thirty days. This is strictly on a donation basis. If the person would like to send a donation to the healer after the thirty days, Nancy sees to it that the Pen Pal Healer receives the money.

To receive Healing Hankies, please provide name, address, and ZIP code. An advanced healing student will fill up two hankies and mail them to you for $5.00.

If you would like to receive a healing from one of the Healing Pen Pals, you can either email Nancy@echobodine.com and in the subject part of your email put Healing Pen Pals, or you can send us a letter at:

Echo Bodine – Healing Pen Pals
P.O. Box 385321
Bloomington, MN 55438

Acknowledgments

To Jude Curran at ACS Publications for putting so much time and effort into getting this book out into the world. To Marc Allen, Georgia Hughes, Marjorie Conte, and Munro Magruder at New World Library for keeping this book alive, giving it brand new energy and a new cover — and for making it the success it's meant to be. Thanks so much for believing in me and the work I do.

God Bless,
Echo

About the Author

Echo Bodine is a renowned psychic, spiritual healer, and teacher. She has appeared on many national television programs, including NBC's *Later Today*, *Sally Jesse Raphael*, *Sightings*, and *The Other Side*. She is the author of several books about psychic and spiritual phenomena, including *Echoes of the Soul; Hands That Heal; A Still, Small Voice; Relax, It's Only a Ghost; The Gift;* and *Dear Echo*. Her radio show in Minnesota on WFMP at FM 107.1 is called *Living with Echo Bodine*.

In addition to classes offered through her teaching and healing center in Bloomington, Echo lectures throughout the country on life, death, life after death, living by intuition, and developing psychic abilities. She can be reached at:

P.O. Box 385321
Bloomington, MN 55438
echo@echobodine.com

Visit Echo's website for information about her books, videos, and tapes:
www.echobodine.com